BOMBER MISSIONS

BOMBER MISSIONS

AVIATION ART OF WORLD WAR II

G.E. Patrick Murray

BARNES & NOBLE

NEW YORK

2006 Barnes & Noble Publishing

ISBN-13: 978-0-7607-8309-2
ISBN-10: 0-7607-8309-8

Printed at KHL Printing in Singapore

1 3 5 7 9 10 8 6 4 2

To Thea and Meg.

The publisher gratefully acknowledges the many talented artists who allowed their work to be included in these pages:

Robert Bailey

Gil Cohen

Jim Dietz

Paul Eckley

Keith Ferris

Nixon Galloway

Henry Godines

Roy Grinnell

Jim Laurier

William S. Phillips

Stan Stokes

Robert Taylor

Nicolas Trudgian

Keith Woodcock

Special thanks also to Art Lumley, executive director of the American Association of Aviation Artists, for his invaluable assistance in contacting the artists represented in this book, and to Colin Heaton for his knowledgeable contributions regarding the pilots of the *Luftwaffe*.

Contents

Introduction

A ten man B-24 crew poses in front of *Pistol Packin' Mama* in 1944. Aircraft nose art reached its height of popularity during World War II, and though it could be found on all types of planes, the bomber was the ideal canvas. Pistol Packin' Mama was a well-used name that appeared on many American aircraft in all theaters.

In November 1932, British Prime Minister Stanley Baldwin warned the House of Commons that there was no defense against bombing, and that "the man in the street ought to know that no power on earth" could prevent him from being bombed. "The bomber will always get through," Baldwin prophesied. Members of Parliament would have remembered that fifteen years earlier the Germans had bombed London, causing a panic in which more than a quarter of a million people fled the city. After his speech, Baldwin traveled to Geneva for a disarmament conference sponsored by the League of Nations where he failed to convince the League to ban the bomber. On the night of May 10–11, 1941, German bombers destroyed the Chamber of the House of Commons.

In the first half of the twentieth century, the strategic bomber evoked as much fear and dread as nuclear missiles did in the second half of the century, and Baldwin's remarks reflected the common wisdom of the day. The common wisdom about bombing, however, was based on assumptions that were nearly all wrong. Most pundits, including Italy's Giulio Duohet, believed that there was no defense against bombers because there was so little difference in the relative performance of bombers and fighters at the time he was writing, in the 1920s; there was a huge difference by 1939. American air power proponent General William "Billy" Mitchell argued in 1925 that bombers would be able to hit "vital centers" in the next war, knocking out such strategic targets as the infrastructure of electrical, water, and gas utilities, bringing city services to a standstill. Mitchell and Duohet greatly overestimated the damage that bombs would cause and greatly underestimated the ability to repair bomb damage. Air Chief Marshal Sir Hugh "Boom" Trenchard, the father of the Royal Air Force (RAF), argued that bombing cities would affect civilian morale to such an extent that the psychological damage would outweigh the physical by twenty to one. Extrapolating the results from World War I led many to exaggerate the impact of bombing in future conflicts. Duohet, for example, believed that one hundred bombers each carrying four thousand pounds (1,814kg) of gas bombs could kill fifty thousand people in ten different cities. All the experts expected that poison gas, along with high explosives and incendiaries, would produce mass panic, and panic would lead governments to surrender. In the end, though, only atomic weapons would fulfill such predictions.

Air forces that attempted strategic bombing throughout much of World War II labored under misconceptions that could be described as naïve at best and negligent at worst, and it was not until the last year of the war that its deadly promise was fulfilled. Reaching its prophesied potential had required more than a decade of advancements in engineering and navigational technology, the industrial mobilization of Britain and the United States, and the personal bravery and sacrifice of hundreds of thousands of air crews.

At the start of World War II, only Britain and the United States had prototypes of four-engine bombers. The first British four-engine design, the Short Stirling, had a wingspan of less than a hundred feet (31m) so that it could fit through the standard British hangar. The Stirling's wingspan limited its lift and the plane's ceiling so that it had to fly through the Alps rather than over them. The most successful British bomber of the war, the four-engine Lancaster, was an outgrowth of a less-than-successful airframe, the twin-engine Manchester, but the Lancasters would not arrive in large numbers until 1943. Until then the British would have to make do with twin-engine models, such as the rugged Vickers Wellington and the ugly Armstrong Whitworth Whitley, otherwise known as the Flying Barn Door. The second British four-engine bomber to enter service was the Handley Page Halifax, which was underpowered and prone to rudder stalls. British bombers had four machine guns in their rear power-operated turrets, but as these were only .303 caliber, they proved no match for German fighters such as the Messerschmitt Me 109 and the Focke Wulf 190, which were armed with cannon as well as machine guns.

The United States Army Air Forces, as the Army Air Corps was officially known after February 1942, entered World War II with two four-engine bomber designs and a third in development. The most famous American bomber of the war was the Boeing B-17 Flying Fortress, which was extremely durable and beautifully designed, but carried a relatively small bomb load. The Consolidated B-24 Liberator was intended as the replacement for the B-17, but it was not as rugged, and hits into its wing produced catastrophic results. The high Davis profile wing gave the Liberator less drag and more speed than the B-17, but it also gave it less stability when damaged. Fitted with a modern tricycle landing gear and a retractable belly turret, the B-24 carried more tonnage and had

BELOW: The Boeing B-17F was one of the United States' standard heavy bombers. The high-altitude, four-engine Flying Fortress was used by the Eighth Air Force in England to bomb targets in Germany during daylight hours. Shown here is *Just-a-Snappin'*, of the 100th Bomb Group.

greater range than the Flying Fortress, but could not fly as high as its four-engine counterpart. The Liberator also saw service as a long-range, anti-submarine warfare plane, because it could fly for thirteen hours and more than 2,500 miles (4,023km). More than 18,000 B-24s were produced, compared to just over 12,700 B-17s. Eventually, the B-17 finished the war with thirteen .50-caliber Browning machine guns, while the B-24 mounted ten.

When World War II began in September 1939, British Prime Minister Neville Chamberlain was initially reluctant to start a strategic bombing campaign. Fearing German retaliation, Chamberlain was wary of being the first to bomb private property and risk civilian lives. Even as the German juggernaut swept across the Low Countries and northern France, the French refused permission to the British to bomb strategic targets, such as factories, or transportation targets in Germany, and even blocked British runways in France with their trucks. The French, too, were certain that their cities would feel the full weight of any reprisal by the German Air Force, the *Luftwaffe*. The French insisted that the British bomb tactical targets instead, such as bridges and armored columns either on or just behind the battlefield. The British used up their obsolete single-engine Fairey Battle bombers and twin-engine Blenheims in these virtual suicide attacks. In an attack on the German bridgehead at Sedan, the RAF lost forty out of seventy-one planes. Days later the RAF's 82 Squadron lost eleven of its twelve Blenheims. The Squadron's commanding officer, Wing Commander

Paddy Bandon, the Earl of Bandon, asked the first and only pilot to land, "Where's everybody else, Morrison?"

Following victory in France, the *Luftwaffe* was totally unprepared to launch a strategic bombing campaign against England. Germany bombed England in the summer of 1940 with a twin-engine bomber force consisting of Heinkel He 111s, Dornier Do 17s, and Junkers Ju 88s, which had been designed to support the ground forces of the German army. Owing to a shortage of bombs in the 1930s, the *Luftwaffe* adopted dive-bombing to increase its accuracy. In order to withstand the stress of dive-bombing, the Germans had to reinforce their twin-engine bombers, which brought about a corresponding decrease in their bomb loads.

Germany's twin-engine bombers lacked the range, bomb-carrying capacity, and armament to engage in a daylight campaign against a determined foe. The RAF's Fighter Command shot down more than 50 percent of Germany's 1,700-plane bomber fleet in the Battle of Britain. Four months later, the Germans switched to night bombing. Over the next ten months of the night campaign, dubbed the Blitz, the Germans killed 40,000 British civilians. Unable to see in the dark, the Germans bombed during the full moon, known as the "bomber's moon," and introduced radio beacon navigation aids such as *X-Gerät* (X-apparatus) for their November 1940 raid on Coventry. Later on, the British learned how to jam the German beams, igniting a scientific war of competing

RIGHT: The cockpit crew of an RAF Whitley twin-engine bomber poses for a picture early in the war. In what were known as "bumf raids," after the British slang for toilet paper, Whitleys dropped propaganda leaflets over Germany in 1939. In 1940 and 1941, they participated in the first raids on Germany and Italy. With primitive intercom and oxygen systems, the Whitley's unpressurized cabins were cold and uncomfortable. BELOW: A *Luftwaffe* briefing somewhere in Poland in 1939 took place on a grass field in front of a Heinkel He 111 bomber. Originally built for Lufthansa, the German airline, as a ten-seat commercial airliner, the He 111 was more suitable as a military craft. Converted to a bomber (the "smoking chamber" on the civilian plane was adapted to be the bomb bay), the He 111 was the muscle of Germany's bomber force in the Battle of Britain.

that bombing Germany would convince the Americans, who were still neutral, that the British were worth supporting. Brave intentions could not change the weather, the industrial pollution of the Ruhr, or the fact that human beings cannot see in the dark. In August 1941 a secret British study, the Butt Report, concluded that only one bomber in five got within five miles of the target (only one in ten over the Ruhr), and that one-half of all bombs fell on open space. Air Ministry officials began to refer to these results as "agricultural bombing."

Unable to find specific targets, in February 1942 the British switched to area bombing, under the delusion that Bomber Command could diminish German morale after the *Luftwaffe* had failed to dent British morale in the Battle of Britain and the Blitz. Within days of that decision, Air Chief Marshal Sir Arthur Harris took over Bomber Command. An obstinate, single-minded man, Harris drew up a list of the fifty-eight largest German cities that Bomber Command would destroy. Harris' staff kept up his so-called Blue Books that contained detailed photographs of the areas his crews had bombed and he showed them to all visitors to his headquarters. The more acreage he could destroy, the sooner he believed he could end the war. In May 1942, Harris launched the first thousand-plane raid on Cologne. By destroying 600 acres (240 ha) of downtown Cologne, Harris scored a major propaganda coup and ended all talk of parceling out his bombers to other commands or services.

When the Eighth United States Air Force arrived in Britain in June 1942, it promised to relieve Bomber Command of the sole burden of bombing Germany, but the British scoffed at the American notion of daylight precision bombing, which they regarded as tantamount to suicide. When the American bombers conducted daylight attacks on targets in France and the rest of occupied Europe escorted by RAF Spitfires, bomber losses were light, and Lieutenant General Ira Eaker, commanding general of the VIII Bomber Command, concluded that B-17s could survive raids deep into Germany. Traveling to North Africa in January 1943, General Eaker convinced Churchill

radio navigation and ranging (radar) devices that alternately aided first the offense, then the defense. On Sunday night, December 29, 1940, a German incendiary attack burned down the City of London, the financial center. While St. Paul's Cathedral was spared, eight other churches built by Sir Christopher Wren following the Great Fire of London in 1666 were destroyed.

Driven off the continent in 1940, the only way for Britain to strike back at Hitler was by bombing. Furthermore, Prime Minister Winston Churchill hoped not to recommend amalgamating the Eighth Air Force into Bomber Command. Instead he urged him to support a plan that would coordinate day and night bombing into an offensive that would bomb Germany "around the clock." Churchill liked the idea and it came to fruition in the Combined Bomber Offensive. By June 1943 the Combined Chiefs of Staff (British and American chiefs acting in tandem) ordered the start of Operation Pointblank, with the German aircraft industry leading the list of targets.

ABOVE: This twenty-one year old sergeant gunner has just returned from the twenty-ninth raid of his Whitley bomber. The young sergeant, a racing motorist before the war, was responsible for earning the painted swastika, which stands for an Me 109 that he shot down from his tail-gun position. The tail gunner was absolutely crucial to the survival of a night-bomber. The key to being a successful tail gunner was to avoid looking down into the spotlights or at the burning cities, and to constantly scan for movement.

One of the first examples of British and American coordination occurred in July and August 1943, when the Eighth Air Force took part in the raids on Hamburg, which was home to Germany's largest lumberyards. Harris employed specially trained crews known as "pathfinders" to find and mark targets, and for the first time employed an antiradar device, code-named Window, which consisted of bundled strips of aluminum foil. Millions of strips were dropped from planes to blind German radar. Lying on the Elbe River less than fifty miles (80.4km) from the North Sea, Hamburg was easy to find and showed up well on H^2S, a ground scanning radar that unlike Gee, an earlier navigation aid, could not be jammed. On the night of July 27–28, 1943, in the second of four raids on Hamburg within nine days, British bombers dropped 1,200 tons (1,080t) of incendiaries in a matter of a few hours. The fires merged to create a firestorm with temperatures reaching 1,300 degrees Fahrenheit (704°C), destroying thirteen square miles (34km^2) and killing more than 40,000 people. Germany's Minister of Armaments, Albert Speer, feared that six more raids like Hamburg would end Germany's war production, but Hamburg was an anomaly that could not be easily repeated. Like the thousand-plane raid on Cologne, however, it was a harbinger of the future.

The raid on Hamburg was a demonstration of what night area attacks could do to Germany's cities. The Americans then launched an attack on August 17, 1943, on Regensburg and Schweinfurt to demonstrate the potential of daylight precision bombing. The P-47 "Thunderbolts" could escort the bombers only as far as the Rhine River, but that did not bother the commanders of the Eighth Air Force. More than 60 percent of Germany's ball bearings came from Schweinfurt, and Eaker and his staff believed that a successful attack had the potential to bring the German army to a grinding halt. Harris, on the other hand, scoffed at what he called "panacea targets," and refused to bomb ball-bearing plants, figuring that the Germans could always find substitutes, which they did. The Eighth Air Force lost sixty bombers out of the 376 dispatched in the twin raid, proving that unescorted bombers could not defend themselves. The 381st Bomb Group lost eleven of its twenty-six planes. Eaker repeated his mistake in mid-October when he sent 291 bombers back to Schweinfurt without long-range escort. While the bombers destroyed more than 65 percent of

RIGHT: The twenty-seven bombs painted on the fuselage of *Hell's Angels* show that it has just returned from its twenty-eighth mission on June 15, 1943. The crew, members of the 303rd Bomb Group, has just finished its tour as well, and their relief is evident. This bomber went on to fly forty-three missions when the average life expectancy of a B-17 in late 1943 was eleven missions. Eventually, a painting of a naked angel with a halo and roller skates was added below the cockpit, aft of the painted bombs.

ball-bearing production, German fighters and flak guns shot down 20 percent of the force, some sixty bombers. It was clear even to Eaker that unescorted bombers were all too vulnerable, and he called off deep raids into Germany. The Eighth desperately needed a long-distance fighter escort.

Being a member of a bomber crew was practically a form of suicide. Airman Ken Stone entered combat with the 381st Bomb Group in mid-June; by October he had survived a loss rate of 72 percent. "Of the nine original crews in our squadron," Stone said, "only two crews completed twenty-five missions." Upon completing twenty-five missions, an Eighth Air Force crewmember got to go

home. In Bomber Command a combat tour was thirty missions, followed by a nine-month tour in Operational Training Units, concluded by a second tour of twenty missions. Less than one-sixth of Bomber Command's crews survived that regimen. By the second half of 1943 the average life span of a British bomber was fourteen missions. John Colville, one of Prime Minister Churchill's private secretaries, flew a Spitfire in 1943 and he described a Bomber Command base: "At this time, November 1943, some 80 percent were failing to complete unscathed their thirty missions. Of courage they had plenty, but there was nothing but lip-biting gloom on those faces."

RIGHT: Polish RAF pilots take some last minute notes of their targets on the continent. During the Battle of Britain, 141 Poles flew for Fighter Command and twenty-nine died for Britain, which was 5 percent of the fighter pilots killed in the battle.

With a disaster on his hands, General Henry H. Arnold, Chief of Staff of the United States Army Air Force, relieved Eaker, replacing him with Lieutenant General James Doolittle. Doolittle had bombed Japan in April 1942 with twin-engine B-25 Mitchell bombers taking off from the deck of the USS *Hornet*. Doolittle also had the good fortune to arrive simultaneously with drop tanks as well as the P-51 Mustang, arguably the greatest piston-engine fighter of World War II. Equipped with 75-gallon (285L) drop tanks and a Rolls-Royce Merlin engine (built on contract by Packard), the P-51 had a top speed of 450 miles per hour (724kph) and could reach Berlin. Arnold's Christmas message of 1943 charged the Eighth Air Force with the destruction of the German Air Force "in the air, on the ground, and in the factories." Beginning on February 20, 1944, Doolittle launched a weeklong series of attacks on German aircraft plants, including Regensburg and Schweinfurt. In the execution of "Big Week" the Eighth Air Force lost three hundred bombers but in the process it dropped nearly 10,000 tons (9,000t) of bombs, more than its entire 1943 total. By the end of February, the German Air Force had lost 33 percent of its fighter aircraft and 20 percent of its pilots. Contrary to expectations, it was the drop tank–equipped P-47 Thunderbolt, that seven-ton (6t) behemoth of a fighter plane with a radial engine and eight .50-caliber machine guns, that flew well beyond the Rhine River and did most of the damage to the German fighters.

Just as the strategic bombers were poised to wreck the German economy, General Dwight D. Eisenhower, the Supreme Allied Commander, adopted the Transportation Plan, which directed the strategic bombers to attack French marshaling yards in order to cripple the French rail system, and with it the German ability to reinforce Normandy. Air Marshal Harris objected strenuously, but discovered to his chagrin that his four-engine Lancasters, with advanced radar and radio navigation systems, bombed marshalling yards at night more accurately than the Eighth Air Force by day. The commander of the U.S. Strategic Air Forces, Lieutenant General Carl A. Spaatz, pushed for his own Oil Plan and won a typical Eisenhower compromise. During good weather the Eighth Air Force bombed Germany's synthetic oil industry and on overcast days it bombed marshaling yards, railroad lines, road cuts, and bridges. Thus, in the period leading up to D-Day, Eisenhower's headquarters actually coordinated Operation Pointblank, unlike the early days of 1943 when the two strategic air forces operated as independent agencies.

Eighty percent of Germany's synthetic fuel came from fourteen plants. Attacks on these plants, especially the huge complex at Meresburg-Leuna, less than twenty miles (32km) west of Leipzig, promised to immobilize the German armed forces. Since 1943, American B-24 Liberators had attacked the major source of German oil, the Ploesti oil refineries in Romania, which by late August 1944 belonged to the Russians. For the first time in the bombing campaign, ULTRA, the code name for intelligence derived from reading German signals traffic, told the Allies that bombing synthetic oil targets was working—the Germans were suffering critical fuel shortages. The Allies listened in as the Germans cut back on flight training and operational flying, and heard when they first dipped into their fuel reserves on June 6, 1944. Much has been made of the increased production of German fighters under the crescendo of Allied bombing, but it is much ado about nothing. As a result of Spaatz's Oil Plan, the German Air Force lacked the aviation fuel to fly the new fighters. By December 1944 the fuel crisis grew so severe that the success of the German Ardennes offensive, the Battle of the Bulge, depended on capturing stocks of American gasoline. In January 1945 a Soviet attack in eastern Germany destroyed 1,300 German tanks that had been immobilized for lack of fuel. After the war, Albert Speer told the Allies that

they had missed an opportunity to end the war earlier by not devoting their maximum effort to the Oil Plan.

The American daylight attacks in early 1944 resulted in the destruction of the German Air Force, especially its day fighters. Soon it was common to see twin-engine night fighters sporting their distinctive Liechtenstein radar antennas attacking daylight bomber formations. By mid-1944 the German fighter aces were nearly all gone, including *Oberleutnant* Egon Mayer, who had originated the head-on attack against B-17s; Mayer had 103 victories and was shot down by a P-47 in March 1944. Bombing reached a crescendo in the last year of the war, when the Allies dropped 72 percent of the total tonnage that fell on Germany in World War II. With the *Luftwaffe* virtually annihilated, much speculation attaches to Hitler's decision to turn the German jet fighter, the Me 262, into a fighter bomber. Many believe that an operational German jet fighter in 1943 might have defeated the bomber offensive. However, if the Germans had actually lengthened the war into August 1945, they, not the Japanese, would have been the recipients of the atomic bomb. As it was, there had been no defense but flak against the British and American attack on Dresden in mid-February 1945—an attack that created a firestorm that needlessly killed at least 50,000 people, to virtually no military purpose. When it was admitted at an off-the-record briefing at Eisenhower's headquarters that the American bombing of Dresden was intended to prevent relief supplies from reaching the city, an Associated Press war correspondent reported that the Allies were engaged in terror bombing. In the wake of the bombing, Churchill backed away from support of Harris, who had planned the raids, telling his chiefs of staff that Dresden raised very serious questions "against the conduct of Allied bombing."

Bombing Germany cost Bomber Command 57,143 personnel, while the American losses were 52,173 killed. The Allies lost thousands of planes turning Germany's fifty largest cities into rubble. After the war the German government calculated that 593,000 Germans had been killed.

Meanwhile, the war in the Pacific continued. Like the crescendo of bombing in Europe, 90 percent of the bombs dropped on Japan fell in the last five months of the war. The weapon employed was the Boeing B-29 Superfortress, which certainly deserved its name. The B-29 was 141 feet (43m) long; its empty weight was 74,500 pounds (33,823kg)—twice the weight of a B-17. Fully loaded, a B-29 weighed 135,000 pounds (61,290kg) and carried a ten-ton (9t) bomb load some 1,500 miles (2,535km) at a cruising speed of more than three hundred miles per hour (483kph); it carried twelve .50-caliber radar-directed guns as well as a 20mm cannon. It also had a fully pressurized cabin so that the crew did not have to wear oxygen masks or the cumbersome layers of leather and heated flying suits that had been necessary in Europe. The plane was so large that it required concrete runways a mile-and-a-half (2.4km) long. Each B-29 cost the United States government $800,000 and the total cost of the B-29 program was three billion dollars—one billion more than the cost of the atomic bomb. Five hundred B-29s were lost in the campaign against Japan at a cost of $44 million.

The first B-29 base was in Kharagpur in West Bengal, in northeastern India. The giant planes flew to Chengtu in Szechwan province, China, to stage for missions against Kyushu and southern Honshu. Each leg of these missions was at least 1,200 miles (1,931km) and consumed between 6,000 and 9,000 gallons (22,713L and 34,069L) of fuel, which had to be flown by cargo planes over the "hump," the name given to the Himalayas. It took up to twelve gallons (45.4L) of fuel to deliver one gallon (3.8L) of fuel. Little wonder that the American Joint Chiefs of Staff directed landings in the Marianas in order to capture Saipan, which was 1,200 miles (1,931km) from Tokyo.

The first commander of the XXI Bomber Command in the Marianas in November 1944 was Brigadier General Haywood Hansell, who had written the original Army Air Corps AWPD-1 (Air War Plan Directive-1). Hansell served directly under General Arnold, who commanded the Twentieth Air Force from Washington, and he was devoted to strategic bombing. He discovered, however, that what worked over Germany would not work over Japan. In essence, the

ABOVE: Lieutenant Paul Eckley poses in front of the star on his B-17 after returning from three grueling days of bombing missions out of Port Moresby, New Guinea. He had not been able to change clothes or bathe in three days and on the way back to Mareeba fell asleep on a pile of parachutes, messing up his hair. Though he looks chipper here, Eckley admits "it was not all fun and games."

American bombers had discovered that the jet stream passed over Japan from west to east at speeds often approaching 200 miles per hour (322kph). A B-29 at 30,000 feet (9,144m) might pass over Japan from west to east at 500 miles per hour—far too fast for the bombs to fall accurately. Or, if the approach was from east to west, the speed would be slowed enough to risk stalling the plane. In fact, the winds that caused havoc with the planes did affect the accuracy of bombing raids. So many bombs fell in Tokyo Bay that a Japanese joke said that the Americans were trying to starve the Japanese by killing all the fish. Arnold grew impatient waiting for Hansell to produce results, so he replaced him with Major General Curtis E. LeMay, a veteran of the bombing of Germany. On learning that LeMay was coming to the Pacific, one squadron commander remarked, "LeMay will get us all killed."

Unlike his predecessor, LeMay was not married to a concept. If high altitude daylight precision bombing would not work, then he would try night area bombing. Night bombing allowed LeMay to send in the B-29s between 6,000 and 9,000 feet (1,829m and 2,743m), which saved gasoline and prevented the massive Curtiss Wright 3350 engines from catching fire, as they often did at high altitudes. It also avoided the Japanese fighters because their night fighters were ineffective. By stripping the B-29 of all its heavy defensive armament except the tail gun, LeMay could load even more incendiaries on each bomber. The Army Air Forces had taken delivery of boatloads of M69 incendiary bombs, which exploded at 2,500 feet (762m) and released thirty-eight incendiary bombs, one for every fifty feet (15.2m). On the night of March 9–10, 1945, some three hundred B-29s dropped 2,000 tons (1,800t) of incendiaries and high explosives on Tokyo—very likely the worst raid in terms of civilian casualties in the history of bombing. Perhaps as many as 110,000 people died in the firestorm that burned out sixteen square miles (41.4sq. km) of the city and destroyed 250,000 buildings. Temperatures were so extreme that water sprayed on the fires vaporized on contact and fire equipment sank into the melted asphalt pavement.

By mid-June 1945, LeMay had burned down all of Japan's major cities and moved on to those with populations between 100,000 and 200,000. Toyoma was 99.5 percent destroyed; one wonders what was left to count. By late July, LeMay had run out of targets. The Twentieth Air Force was dropping 100,000 tons (90,000t) of incendiaries and high explosives each month on Japan's cities. A vastly more powerful bomb that combined the blast effects of high explosives with the incendiary effects of firebombs waited in the wings.

On the island of Tinian, Colonel Paul W. Tibbets, Jr., commanded the 509th Composite Group, which had practiced special tactics for a mission to drop a bomb of unusual force. Major Charles W. Sweeney's 393rd Bombardment Squadron provided most of the men and the planes. Tibbets waited until August 4 to brief his crews on their mission; he omitted telling them that they would be dropping an atomic bomb. On August 6, 1945, Tibbets took off from Tinian for the six and a half hours it would take for the *Enola Gay* to reach Hiroshima. A naval ordnance expert assembled the bomb's trigger in mid-flight to prevent an unintentional detonation in the event of a crash on takeoff. The bomb dropped on Hiroshima was a uranium bomb nicknamed "Little Boy." At 8:15 A.M. the bomb-bay doors opened and moments later the bomb was released. Fifty seconds later "Little Boy" exploded at 1,900 feet (680m), producing a blast with a force of more than 15,000 tons (13,608t) of TNT; at the center of the explosion, the temperature reached 5,400 degrees Fahrenheit (2,982°C). Three days later, on August 9, Major Charles Sweeney dropped the plutonium weapon, "Fat Man," on Nagasaki from a B-29 named *Bock's Car*. Unlike at Hiroshima, there was no firestorm at Nagasaki, so the casualties were about half that of the Hiroshima bombing. "Fat Man" exploded with a force later estimated at 22,000 tons (19,800t) of TNT, but the bomb landed behind a ridgeline that shielded the city from much of the effects of the blast and radiation. The most recent statistics list 70,000 killed in Hiroshima and 36,000 dead in Nagasaki with an equal number injured in both cities. The final number of dead could easily have reached 200,000 because the radiation caused leukemia and other cancers

that killed people for years to follow. Nearly four square miles (10sq. km) were completely devastated in Hiroshima and one and one-half square (4sq. km) miles were destroyed in Nagasaki.

Such was the ultimate legacy of strategic bombing, as anticipated by the dire prophecies of the twenties and thirties. Analysts have since determined that 2,000 tons (1,800t) of incendiaries would have produced the same results, but delivering such a load would have required three hundred B-29s rather than two planes per raid. In the process of dropping 170,000 tons (153,000t) of bombs on Japan over the course of fifteen months, the Twentieth Air Force casualties numbered more than three thousand killed, wounded, and missing. The strategic bomber ushered in the atomic age, and humans have lived for the past half-century under the threat of weapons of mass destruction that were dropped upon hundreds of thousands of people.

ABOVE: The crew of the *Enola Gay*, standing from left to right: Lieutenant Colonel John Porter; Major Theodore J. Van Kirk; Major Thomas W. Ferebee; Colonel Paul W. Tibbets, Jr.; Captain Robert A. Lewis; Lieutenant Jacob Beser. Kneeling from left to right: Sergeant Joseph Stiborik; Sergeant George R. Caron; Private First Class Richard H. Nelson; Sergeant Robert H. Shumard; Sergeant Wyatt E. Duzenbury.

Assault on the Capital

German Air Force

Robert Taylor

IT WAS SEPTEMBER 7, 1940, AND GERMAN BOMBERS HAD BEEN INFLICTING NEAR CRIPPLING losses on Royal Air Force aerodromes. But this day would see the Germans change their tactics and begin bombing London—a misjudgment that would save RAF's Fighter Command and cost the *Luftwaffe* the Battle of Britain. The German attack began at four in the afternoon and continued for almost twelve hours, setting fire to the London docks and killing more than three hundred people. It also marked the beginning of the Blitz, the night bombing of the capital that continued until May 1941.

Assault on the Capital features the fighters and bombers of the *Luftwaffe* and depicts the action of that September afternoon. In the foreground, a German Me 109 flown by Herbert Ihlefeld, who himself shot down an RAF Hurricane that day, escorts two Ju 88s. Ihlefeld commanded an operational training unit that has just driven off Hurricanes of the RAF's 242 Squadron, but not before the Hurricanes hit the lead Ju 88, which is already smoking and will not return. A formation of German twin-engine Heinkel He 111s trails in the background, flying under a rain of flak.

The Germans took on the world's largest city with a twin-engine medium bomber force that numbered about 1,400 planes. German twin-engine bombers had small bomb loads, about one-ton (0.9t) for the Heinkel and two-tons (1.8t) for the Junkers; it was impossible to hurt a city of London's magnitude with such a bomber force. Built to provide tactical support for the German army, the Me 109 had only ten minutes of flight time over London before it had to return to its bases in France. Consequently unable to protect their bombers from heavy daylight losses, the Germans switched to night operations. Losses of German bombers approached 70 percent over the summer months, and the *Luftwaffe* would go on to lose more bombers from accidents than it did to enemy action. Before every mission, *Oberst* (Colonel) Johannes Fink of *Kampfgeschwader* II (Bomb Wing II) would give his crews this chilling advice: "You must make your wills!"

Circus Outbound

United States Army Air Force

Keith Ferris

THE 93RD BOMBARDMENT GROUP WAS COMMANDED BY COLONEL EDWARD "TED" J. Timberlake from March 1942 to May 1943. Having bombed France, hunted U-boats in the Bay of Biscay, and been stationed in North Africa, the group was given the nickname "Ted's Travelling Circus." It was the oldest B-24 group in the Eighth Air Force and had the lowest operational losses of all six bomb groups within VIII Bomber Command.

Here, the B-24s are depicted climbing to 21,000 feet (6,400m) on March 18, 1943, on the way to bomb submarine pens at Vegesack, Germany, on the Weser River. The yellow "C" on the tail of the plane in front is the individual identification marking of the aircraft within its squadron. The eight yellow bombs on its nose show that the bomber is on its ninth mission. Cut into the encircled star on the fuselage is the left waist machine gun position. Manipulating this sixty-four pound (29kg) .50-caliber machine gun in a two hundred mile-per-hour (322kph) slipstream required brute strength, and much training was needed to be able to hit a German fighter with deflection fire. American gunners lodged inflated hit claims because often seven or eight gunners believed that they had shot down the same plane. In October 1942, American gunners claimed to have downed 102 fighters over France, but that was later downgraded to fifty-seven. After the war, German records revealed that they had lost only two planes that day. Several months after this raid, the 93rd traveled to Libya to take part in the raid on the Ploesti oilfields in Romania. Fifteen of the eighteen bombers shown here were lost.

First Mission/July 4th 1942

United States Army Air Force

Nixon Galloway, ASAA

BRIGADIER GENERAL IRA EAKER, COMMANDING GENERAL OF THE VIII BOMBER COMMAND in High Wycombe, outside of London, ordered the first American raid on occupied Europe for Independence Day, July 4, 1942. The mission employed twelve RAF Boston IIIs (American A-20s) borrowed from No. 226 Squadron. Six RAF crews joined six American crews from the American 15th Bomb Squadron training at Swanton Morley and took off to bomb German airfields on the Dutch coast. Orders were to fly at thirty feet (9m) and turn with rudder control rather than banking so as to deny German flak towers a full profile target.

Flying the second RAF Boston to bomb the airfield at DeKooy, Captain Charles C. Kegelman came in at the prescribed altitude when German flak tore off the propeller of the plane's right engine. The right wing hit the ground; then the fuselage bounced off the ground. Kegelman maintained control of the plane, turned with rudder control, shot out a flak tower, and returned safely to base. The plane behind him banked to turn and the German gunners shot it down. For his skill and heroism, Kegelman received the Distinguished Service Cross (DSC) while the bombardier and two gunners received the Distinguished Flying Cross (DFC). Kegelman was killed in the crash of a B-25 Mitchell bomber in the Philippines late in the war.

Arctic Encounter

German Air Force

Robert Bailey

PRIME MINISTER WINSTON CHURCHILL AND PRESIDENT FRANKLIN D. Roosevelt insisted on using Arctic convoys to deliver American Lend-Lease supplies to Soviet ports on the Barents and the White Seas. For the crews who manned these convoys in the summer of 1942, it was a game of Russian roulette played in perpetual daylight against German surface ships, submarines, and airplanes. Convoy PQ-17 left Iceland for Murmansk on June 27. Based on an ULTRA intercept warning of a German surface attack by the battleship *Tirpitz*, the sister ship of the *Bismarck*, and the pocket battleship *Lützow*, Admiral Sir Dudley Pound, the First Sea Lord, ordered the convoy to scatter and its escort to sail to the west. That decision doomed PQ-17 to incessant air and submarine attacks. Ironically, the German naval contingent put back to port when several destroyers ran aground in shallow Norwegian waters. When the German fleet did not sortie, it was Pound's order to scatter that doomed the convoy.

On July 5, 1942, Ju 88s from *Kampfgeschwader* 30, including the one flown by *Oberst* (Colonel) Hajo Hermann, demonstrated their dive-bombing capabilities, sinking several of PQ-17's unescorted bulk cargo carriers shown here. Ultimately, the convoy lost twenty-four ships. Hermann and his fellow bomber pilots sank eight, U-boats sank nine, and the two forces combined to sink another seven ships. Losses included more than 3,800 trucks, 400 tanks, 2,500 planes, and 153 seaman drowned or frozen in 37° Fahrenheit (2.7°C) water. Only eleven of the original convoy made it safely to Murmansk, and Churchill suspended the convoys for two months until more escort vessels were available.

Legendary *Luftwaffe* pilot Major Hajo Hermann, an innovative tactician and veteran of more than three hundred bombing missions, sank 70,000 tons (63,503t) of shipping as a bomber pilot during the war.

Robert Bailey A.S.A.A. ©1998

The Red Gremlin

United States Army Air Force

William S. Phillips

THE *RED GREMLIN* FLEW GENERAL DWIGHT D. EISENHOWER FROM ENGLAND TO GIBRALTAR where he commanded Operation Torch, the Allied invasion of North Africa, on November 8, 1942. Bad weather prevented Eisenhower's departure on November 2 and 3. By November 4, Eisenhower ordered his pilot, Major Paul W. Tibbets, Jr., to take off in rain and fog despite Tibbets' misgivings. The six B-17s that flew Eisenhower and his staff were from the 97th Bomb Group at Hurn, England, on the south Channel coast. Coincidentally, the 97th Bomb Group provided the basis for the novel and the 1949 motion picture, *Twelve O'clock High*. Following the eight-hour, 1,200-mile (1,931km) flight, the arrival in Gibraltar of *The Red Gremlin* went unreported in London for several hours after it landed, leading to a flurry of teletypes until Eisenhower's whereabouts could be certified. One of the five B-17s that took off with Eisenhower's plane disappeared and was never found. A sixth plane, carrying Major General James Doolittle, hero of the B-25 raid on Tokyo in April 1942, developed brake trouble and barely missed crashing into *The Red Gremlin* while they both taxied in the fog, a collision which would likely have led to fire and explosion, and the death of all onboard. After repairs to Doolittle's plane, it arrived in Gibraltar a day later, but only after surviving a battle with four Ju 88s that made repeated head-on attacks. Eisenhower went on to become the Supreme Allied Commander of Operation Overlord, Doolittle later became the commander of the Eighth Air Force, and Tibbets dropped the first atomic bomb on Hiroshima.

124444

THE RED GREMLIN

PAUL TIBBETS   Tom Ferebee   Dutch Van Kirk   Herman Haag   CHARLIE PEACH   ZACK COWAN

No Flying Today
United States Army Air Force

William S. Phillips

WILLIAM S. PHILLIPS EVOKES A SENSE OF CALM DURING A SNOWSTORM THAT HAS GROUNDED both hawk and bomber. The weather has closed in on Framlingham, England, an historic market town in Suffolk and home of the 596th Squadron of the 390th Bomb Group, Eighth Air Force. The large J on the B-17's tail indicates that it belongs to the 390th Bomb Group.

Bad weather, rain, and clouds posed a major problem to daylight precision bombing, and snow cancelled operations entirely. Daylight precision bombing seemed like a good idea when practiced over American airfields in the desert Southwest, but Europe is cloud-covered 85 percent of the time. Attacks on oil, aircraft, power, and armament targets required good weather. American air staffs concluded that Italy would have better weather than England, so the Army Air Forces established the Fifteenth United States Air Force in Foggia, Italy. The assumption was that from November 1943 to May 1944 heavy bombers would be able to operate fifty-five days in Italy compared to thirty-one days in England, but the assumption proved overly pessimistic. The Eighth Air Force in England was operational on ninety-four days, while the Fifteenth Air Force in Italy flew bomber missions on 102 days. Both the aircrews and the Germans welcomed bad weather as a respite from the nerve-wrenching experience of bombing.

Mauled by a Marauder

United States Army Air Force

Stan Stokes

PLACING ITS WING AT THE SHOULDER OF THE FUSELAGE GAVE THE B-26 MARTIN MARAUDER huge bomb bays, allowing it to carry as much bomb tonnage as a B-17. The plane's wingspan was a mere sixty-five feet (9.8m), which made it difficult to handle, especially with a heavy bomb load. The B-26 required 2,500-foot (762m) runways to take off and land, which it did at 130 miles-per-hour (209kph)—about the same speed as a modern jet fighter. Initially, the plane's engines proved troublesome: if one engine quit, the plane tended to flip over and crash. B-26 training took place at MacDill Field in Florida, and its many accidents led crews to coin the phrase, "One a day in Tampa Bay." When Martin lengthened the wing span to seventy-one feet (22m), the B-26 stopped killing inexperienced crews. Although never an easy plane to fly, especially when limited to one engine, the B-26 became the safest American aircraft in the European Theater; its loss rate per sortie was 0.3 percent.

Given the plane's checkered past, the incident depicted here by Stan Stokes was remarkable. On November 29, 1943, Captain Pete LaFramboise of the 386th Bomb Group, Ninth Air Force, has feathered the left engine of *Sexation* over France. Fw 190s have knocked out one engine and the hydraulic system, and the plane has lost speed and altitude. The Marauder, however, mounted eleven .50-caliber machine guns in the nose, the fuselage, the dorsal turret, and the tail, and two in its lower waist, below the national insignia. As LaFramboise struggled to fly *Sexation*, Sgt. Bill Norris, the tail gunner, shot down the Focke Wulf; its pilot is seen standing in the cockpit. Norris shot down three German fighters that day, making him the "top gun" of the 386th Bomb Squadron. Because of the damaged hydraulic system, LaFramboise could not lower the landing gear, but he brought his crew home by belly-landing. He and Norris both received the Silver Star for their skill and heroism.

Robert Bailey A.S.A.A. ©1999

Night Crossing

German Air Force

Robert Bailey

FOLLOWING THE ATTACK ON HAMBURG IN JULY AND AUGUST 1943, *REICHSMARSCHALL* Hermann Göring held a conference with top *Luftwaffe* officers and leaders of the German aircraft industry to address the national emergency. Göring wanted to adopt defensive measures to protect Germany from Allied bombing, but Adolf Hitler turned him down flat, saying, "Terror can only be broken with terror." The German *Führer* demanded more bombers, not fighters, and he said that the German people were losing faith in their Air Force. Unless something was done to bomb England, Hitler warned, the people would go mad. After his meeting with Hitler, Göring put his head down on a desk and sobbed.

Göring's response to Hitler's tirade was to name *Oberst* (Colonel) Dieter Peltz *Angriffsführer* England (Attack Leader England) and to order the *Luftwaffe* to return to bombing England at night, as if it were 1940–1941 all over again. Beginning in January and ending in April 1944, the Germans launched fourteen raids against London, as well as bombing Hull, Bristol, and South Wales. Londoners called it "the little Blitz." George Orwell noted, "There are air raid alarms almost every night but hardly any bombs." In February 1944, the Germans killed a thousand Londoners. On February 20–21, they hit government buildings at Whitehall, blowing out all the windows in the War Office and at 10 Downing Street, the home of the Prime Minister.

Robert Bailey portrays a low-level attack by a Dornier Do 217 in early 1944. Although blackout regulations would have been in effect and there would have been blackout curtains on the train and in the station, Bailey leaves the lights on to give us a better glimpse of the action. This Dornier was a revamped version of the Do 17 that had bombed England in the summer of 1940. The Do 217 was longer and weighed 19,985 pounds (9,065kg), carried a two-ton (1.8t) bomb load, and had a range of 1,550 miles (2,500km). But all of this emphasis on producing bombers came at the expense of fighters to protect Germany.

Liberators

United States Army Air Force

Stan Stokes

OWING TO ITS COMBINATION OF SIZE, SPEED, AND RANGE, THE CONSOLIDATED B-24 Liberator was the most versatile American bomber. The British not only gave the plane its name, they eventually employed five squadrons of Liberators in anti-submarine warfare. Liberators performed superbly in the anti-submarine patrol. Flying at between 1,500 and 2,000 feet (457m and 610m), B-24s could patrol for three hours some 1,100 miles (1,770km) from their bases. In comparison the British Sunderland flying boat was limited to two hours at six hundred miles (966km) from its base and the American Catalina flying boat could maintain station for three hours while eight hundred miles (1,287 km) from its base. From bases in Newfoundland, Nova Scotia, Iceland, and Northern Ireland, allied aircraft were able to cover most of the Atlantic Ocean by August 1942. However, the range of available aircraft left a gap south of Iceland and north of the Azores.

In February 1943, President Franklin D. Roosevelt requested Admiral Ernest J. King, chief of naval operations, to report on how many VLR (Very Long Range) Liberators were in the Atlantic—there were fourteen. Following the Washington Convoy Conference of March 1943, Roosevelt ordered King to transfer some of the Pacific Liberators to the Atlantic theater to close the so-called air gap. By April 1943 there were forty-one VLR Liberators operating from Atlantic bases.

Army Air Forces crews were not trained for long-range flying over vast stretches of ocean. The job was boring at times, but it called for expert navigation, and eventually the job fell to the United States Navy. B-24s could carry up to twenty-four depth charges for use against German submarines. More importantly, by closing the air gap the Liberators denied German submarines the luxury of recharging their batteries on the surface during daylight hours. By mid-1943, Liberators equipped with airborne radar and spotlights, known as Leigh lights, also made it fatal for submarines to be on the surface at night.

After the Mission

United States Army Airforce

Gil Cohen

ALL BOMBER CREWS WENT THROUGH INTERROGATION FOLLOWING THEIR MISSIONS. THESE post-combat interviews yielded critical information about enemy tactics and targets, the number and types of fighters, and where the flak was light or heavy. The Germans concentrated their flak to protect their most important targets. Though flak could never be entirely avoided, by locating the gun concentrations it would be possible to approach targets from less dangerous flight paths.

Gil Cohen captures the anxiety and relief that merged in the moment. Nearly all of the men drink coffee or smoke, the memory of their mission still fresh in their minds. The RAF liaison officer smokes a pipe while the Americans smoke Lucky Strikes or Camels. The navigator lights a Lucky Strike from one of the new red packs using his Zippo lighter. The pre-war package had been green but the new packs carried the slogan "Lucky Strike green has gone to war." The green dye was used for the war effort. The waist gunner has a bandage on his wounded hand and he still wears his parachute harness, earphones, and oxygen mask. Next to the waist gunner the bombardier rubs his neck and examines the map where the pilot points out a geographical feature of the raid. The bombardier wears his yellow life preserver, known as a "Mae West" because it blew up in the front; it is dated 5/2/43. Glancing out the window of the Quonset hut, the tail gunner witnesses the safe return of another bomber. Model aircraft hang from the ceiling, and on the wall are silhouettes of German aircraft and advice on "How to Bail Out of the Flying Fortress." The airman in the left background looks like a man coming to terms with death. These men depict what Jack Colville called "lip-biting gloom."

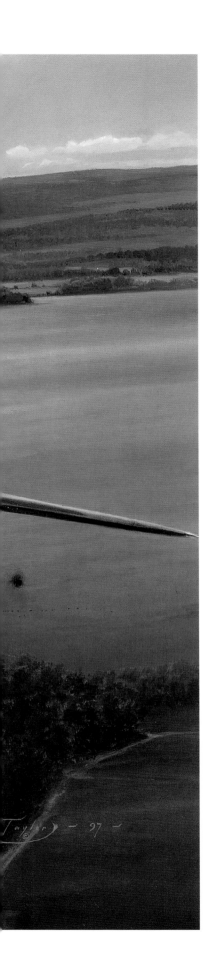

Operation Chastise

Royal Air Force

Robert Taylor

ON THE NIGHT OF MAY 16–17, 1943, NINETEEN LANCASTERS FROM BOMBER
Command's No. 617 Squadron, led by Wing Commander Guy Gibson, attacked
three Ruhr area dams: the Möhne, the Eder, and the Sorpe. They breached the
Möhne and Eder dams but the Sorpe dam survived unscathed. After months of
training for low level attacks, No. 617 Squadron dropped the unique 10,000-
pound (4,536kg) depth-charge bombs designed by British engineer Dr. Barnes
Wallis. Wallis had designed the Wellington bomber and would go on to design
the 10,000-pound (4,536kg) "Tallboy" and the 22,000-pound (9,979kg) "Grand
Slam" bombs.

In *Operation Chastise*, we witness the breaching of the Möhne dam by Flight
Lieutenant "Dinghy" Young. (Young was so named because he had bailed out
twice over the English Channel and ended up in a dinghy.) Gibson's plane is off
to the left, flying through a barrage of defensive fire. In the foreground is the
Lancaster of Australian Flight Lieutenant Harold "Mickey" Martin, later Air
Marshal Sir Harold Martin. Gibson's pilots had practiced bombing at low altitude in order to place Wallis' skip bomb against the wall of the dam where it
would sink and, at the preset depth, explode and crack the dam. To guide the
planes, each Lancaster was fitted with two searchlights that crossed each other at
sixty feet, the precise altitude from which to drop the skip bomb. The breaching
of the two dams drowned 1,300 Germans as well as 750 Russian prisoners of
war, not to mention 6,500 cattle and pigs.

The King and Queen presented Gibson with the Victoria Cross, the highest
British medal given for gallantry; five men earned the DSO (Distinguished
Service Order); and ten men won the DFC (Distinguished Flying Cross). Eight
of the nineteen planes were lost, including some of the best pilots in Bomber
Command. Gibson was killed in a crash later in the war, but the legend of the
"Dambusters" lives on.

Ploesti: Out of the Fire and Fury

United States Army Air Force

William S. Phillips

PLOESTI, ROMANIA, WAS THE IDEAL TARGET FOR PRECISION BOMBING BECAUSE IT SUPPLIED 40 percent of Germany's fuel during the war. En route to raid the oil refineries of Ploesti, two B-24s carrying the primary and deputy navigators of the mission inexplicably crashed into the Mediterranean, off the coast of Greece. Brigadier General Uzal G. Ent, bomber commander Ninth Air Force, flew with Colonel Keith Compton, commander 376th Bomb Group. Ent and Compton took over navigation responsibilities following the death of the lead navigator and mistook Targovista for Floresti, despite strong protests from their junior navigator that they were headed to Bucharest rather than Ploesti. When Ent realized his error and turned back towards the target, he forced two bomb groups to fly through the worst flak surrounding Ploesti, as well as through the smoke and fire of the previous bombing.

Colonel Leon Johnson's 44th Bomb Squadron did not follow the same mistaken path, thanks to Colonel James T. Posey, who found the checkpoint leading to Brazi, the high-octane plant five miles (8km) north of Ploesti. Johnson personally led his squadron as formation commander, flying in the co-pilot's seat of *Susy-Q*, while Major William Brandon piloted the plane. When Johnson found that his target had already been bombed, he directed the squadron to alternate targets.

William S. Phillips portrays the bomb bay doors of the B-24 in their open position, raised up on the side of the plane's fuselage. This door design created less drag than the standard bomb bay doors that opened out. Multiple fires blaze in the background as *Susy-Q* hunts undamaged targets. Brandon won the Distinguished Service Cross for his part in the battle, and Colonel Johnson received the Medal of Honor, making him one of five men to earn it for the Ploesti mission.

Operation Tidal Wave
United States Army Air Force

Nicolas Trudgian

WHEN THE B-24S OF THE 98TH BOMB GROUP, LED BY COLONEL JOHN R. "KILLER" KANE, took a wrong turn on the way to Ploesti, they located their target by following the path of two railroad tracks. In the process, they flew over what they took to be a freight train. The freight train turned out to be a German flak train in disguise, cleverly placed there for just such an eventuality. It immediately dropped its false sides and opened up on the bombers. The flak train forced the aerial gunners to spend precious ammunition dueling with antiaircraft gunners rather than fighter planes. While finding their way to Ploesti, the 98th lost fifteen planes to flak, which the Germans had set to point-blank range.

Trudgian depicts the smoke, fire, flak, and confusion of the mission, with bombers dodging and weaving through the maelstrom. In the background, a B-24 trails smoke and will not survive; in the foreground, *Sandman* has just exited the target area at extremely low altitude. The mistaken approaches of the bomber force threw the plan of attack into confusion. Bombers that flew through the fire and smoke searching for targets risked being blown apart by the delayed-action bombs dropped by their colleagues. And they flew so low, below two hundred feet (61m), that they risked smashing into smokestacks or the cables of barrage balloons. Of the 178 bombers that took part in the raid, fifty-four were lost, forty-one to enemy action—a loss rate more than 30 percent. The raid knocked out some parts of the Ploesti complex for six months, some for a year or more, and others for the duration of the war. But since Ploesti had been operating at only 60 percent capacity at the time of the raid, the Germans simply put unused capacity back into production. Thus the actual loss to the Germans was not 40 percent as claimed by General Brereton but more like 2 percent. Within weeks, the plant was producing more product than before the raid. The losses to the Ninth Air Force were so severe that it would be eight months before the bombers returned to Ploesti.

Coming Home/England 1943
United States Army Air Force

Gil Cohen

COMING HOME/ENGLAND 1943 RECREATES THE RETURN OF THE *KAYO KATY* CREW TO their base in England. The work is evocative of the motion picture *Twelve O'clock High*, made from Colonel Beirne Lay, Jr.'s novel, which was based on the exploits of the Eight Air Force's 97th Bomb Group stationed at Polebrook and Grafton Underwood. It has rained and the skies are overcast as the bombers return to base. The ambulance in the background shows that there are wounded aboard the B-17, and there is one plane missing from the formation of five flying overhead.

The pilot, having his cigarette lit, resembles Gregory Peck, who played tough disciplinarian General Frank Savage in *Twelve O'clock High*. A tail gunner and the waist gunners exit at the rear of the aircraft. In the right foreground, one airman carries his sizeable parachute. A ground crewman, who has just arrived on his bicycle, points to holes in the inboard engine nacelle, which is missing part of its outer covering. Damage to the right front of the plane is visible below the navigator's window. Above this window, yellow bombs grouped in fives signify that the plane's crew had completed twenty-two missions prior to this one; ground crew will soon add the twenty-third. At twenty-five missions the crew will have defied the odds and completed its tour, and will get to go home.

Statistics kept on 2,051 Eighth Air Force aircrews show that the odds were not in their favor. Only 27 percent, some 559, finished twenty-five missions, while 1,195 (58 percent) were killed. Nearly 16 percent suffered burns, frostbite, wounds, or the psychological effects of combat and were lost to the service. On average, 4 percent were killed on every mission. Statistically, the average number of missions completed for the entire cohort was sixteen.

Mission Regensburg

United States Army Air Force

Gil Cohen

Harry H. Crosby, lead navigator of *Just-a-Snappin'*, flew thirty-seven missions during the war and retired as a Lieutenant Colonel. He went on to write a memoir entitled *A Wing and a Prayer* about his experiences in the "Bloody Hundredth."

GIL COHEN TAKES US INSIDE *JUST-A-SNAPPIN*, A B-17F FROM THE 418TH BOMB Squadron, 100th Bomb Group, on the infamous August 17, 1943, mission against the Messerschmitt factory at Regensburg, Germany. The bombardier, Lieutenant James R. Douglass, signals the navigator, Lieutenant Harry H. Crosby, who notes the exact time of bomb release. The temperature inside the unpressurized plane dropped to -40° Fahrenheit (-40.5°C). As seen here, crews wore oxygen masks, earphones, scarves, flying helmets, sun goggles, heated flying gloves, flying suits, fleece-lined leather jackets, and parachute harnesses. Parachutes were too bulky for the tight confines so they were stored and snapped to the harnesses for quick retrieval. Underneath their flying suits, crews wore long underwear, another electrically heated flying suit, several pairs of socks and winter flying socks, heated flying shoes inside heavy flying boots, and silk gloves under their heated gloves.

Regensburg was part of a two-pronged mission. The first wave would fly unescorted past Aachen for three hundred miles (483km) to Regensburg on the Danube and then on to Bône, Algeria, nearly nine hundred miles (1,448km) distant, so they would not have to run the gauntlet of German fighters twice. The Schweinfurt raiders, also unescorted, were to follow fifteen minutes after and attack the ball-bearing complex at Schweinfurt on the Main River while the German Air Force was dealing with the attack on Regensburg. The assumption behind the plan was that unescorted B-17s could defend themselves.

Colonel Curtis LeMay led the Regensburg force. Because of bad weather, LeMay's bombers took off on instruments; time was crucial because his force had to land during daylight in North Africa. Weather also delayed the takeoff of the Schweinfurt raiders for three and a half hours. The Regensburg force lost thirty bombers out of the 144 that bombed the target; the 100th Bomb Group lost ten planes, a hundred men. Because the Schweinfurt force was so late, the German Air Force attacked it going in and coming out and shot down thirty-six of its 230 bombers. Including the planes that landed but would never fly again, the Eighth Air Force lost 147 planes in one day, and six hundred crewmen.

Robert Bailey A.S.A.A. ©1999

Men of the Century

United States Air Force

Robert Bailey

ARTIST ROBERT BAILEY DEPICTS THE TAKEOFF OF THE 100TH BOMB GROUP FROM Thorpe Abbots in Norfolk on October 8, 1943 for a raid against Bremen, Germany. An unnamed B-17 has just left the runway while, in the background, *Holy Terror, Queen Bee,* and *Marie Helena* taxi past the tower. By this time, the group had gained a reputation as a hard-luck outfit and had been given the unfortunate moniker, "The Bloody Hundredth." Losses in the 100th, while not the highest of the Eighth Air Force, tended to come many at a time. The 100th had flown "coffin corner," or low squadron, on the Regensburg raid. Of the three formations (low, medium, high), the low squadron characteristically suffered the highest losses.

The lead aircraft of the 100th Group was *Just a-Snappin*. Hit by flak, it was shot out of formation over the target and went into a flat spin, which pilot Captain Everett Blakely managed to pull out of after dropping three thousand feet (914m) on three engines. The crew destroyed five German planes (Me 109, Me 110, Ju 88, Me 210), but not before the flying German menagerie put nearly a thousand holes into the plane and knocked out another engine. *Just a-Snappin* crash-landed on the shores of East Anglia on two engines with no brakes— remarkably, both pilots survived. All told, the Eighth Air Force lost thirty bombers; seven were from the Bloody Hundredth, including the *Marie Helena* (H-EP), seen taxiing on the extreme left of the painting.

Escorting the Yank

United States Army Air Force

Roy Grinnell

NECESSITY BECAME VIRTUE WHEN AN RAF SPITFIRE ESCORTED A MORTALLY WOUNDED B-17G to an RAF Bomber Command airfield. The Spitfire shows off the rounded wing shape that made it the most beautiful fighter design of World War II. An RAF ground crewman looks up from polishing the Perspex covering of the Lancaster's dorsal power turret. The focus of the work, however, is on the approaching B-17, and even though the incident is fictional, Roy Grinnell's realistic depiction brings to life an event that occured numerous times during the bombing campaign. The Flying Fortress has lost its right outboard engine, and the right inboard engine is on fire and trailing smoke. Feathering that engine at this altitude would risk loss of control and a certain fatal crash. The plane has most likely lost its hydraulic system as well because only the

left wheel is down, the bomb bay doors are still open, and the twin .50-caliber Browning machine guns of the ball turret are pointing downward. Ordinarily, the ball turret would be stowed for landing and the machine guns would be pointing aft toward the plane's tail. Could the ball gunner be fatally injured inside his turret? Unless the plane was very low on fuel, the friction of the bomb bay and the ball turret's machine-gun barrels would create sufficient sparks to make fire a certainty. B-17 crews often survived such landings, but the planes were usually total losses and had to be written off as scrap. Grinnell's scene epitomizes the sense of camaraderie and cooperation between the two aviation giants of World War II.

Incredible 305th

United States Army Air Force

Jim Dietz

ON OCTOBER 14, 1943, THE EIGHTH AIR FORCE WENT BACK TO SCHWEINFURT AND ITS ball-bearing factories. Again the planners divided the force into two separate waves to complicate German fighter defense, but this also meant that the second wave of B-17s would have to bomb through the smoke and dust created by the first. Artist Jim Dietz immortalizes the run up to Schweinfurt by the 305th Bomb Group, which unfortunately had to fly the risky low formation in the first wave. What's particularly interesting about Dietz's painting is what is not seen—there are no American fighters. The battle was entirely one of B-17s versus single and twin-engine fighters.

From the base at Chevelston, fifteen B-17Fs took off. One aborted and returned to base and fourteen flew on, but twelve went down in flames before their crews ever saw Schweinfurt. A rocket from an Me 110 twin-engine, split-tailed fighter blew up one B-17 from the 305th directly over Schweinfurt. German single-engine machines—Me 109s and Fw 190s—led head-on attacks on the B-17Fs to kill the pilots and break up the formations. The B-17G with twin .50-caliber machine guns in a chin turret would soon replace the F models to protect against such attacks. Less maneuverable twin-engine Me 110s fired rockets from the flanks and attacked obliquely. The twin-engine plane at the top center of the picture is an Me 210. Following the raid, only two bombers from the 305th returned to Chevelston. Thirteen ground crews stared in numb disbelief.

Out of 257 B-17s in the bomber force, 197 returned to England, but five crash-landed. Of those 192 remaining aircraft, 142 were damaged. Only fifty planes out of 257 escaped damage. The American doctrine of unescorted bombing into the heart of Germany also died that day. When President Roosevelt let slip to reporters that the Eighth Air Force had lost sixty bombers, the day became known as "black Thursday." General Arnold, chief of staff of the Army Air Forces, decided to replace Eaker at Eighth Air Force with Lieutenant General James Doolittle from the Mediterranean theater. At a post-combat debriefing in England one interrogator asked a crewman, "Any comments?" and the man answered, "Yeah. Jesus Christ, give us some fighters for escort!"

DIETZ

The Bait Bites Back

United States Army Air Force

William S. Phillips

THE MARTIN B-26 MARAUDER CLEARLY OWED ITS CONTINUED PRODUCTION TO BRIGADIER General James "Jimmy" Doolittle. When a series of fatal training accidents threatened its future, the Chief of Staff of the United States Army Air Forces, Lieutenant General Henry H. "Hap" Arnold, ordered Doolittle to look into the plane's record. The first thing Doolittle did was to fly to Baltimore to see the officials at Martin. Afterwards he went to Marauder training sites and listened to the complaints from B-26 crews. The men who flew the Marauder were clearly apprehensive. They said that the plane would not take off on one engine and it could not make a turn into a "dead" engine, that is, an engine that has been shut down.

Always one of the best pilots in the service, Doolittle set out to redeem the reputation of the plane that the crews called the "Flying Prostitute" or the "Baltimore Whore." Both of those names refer to the plane's short wingspan, which crews said left it "without any visible means of support." Doolittle taxied a B-26 without a co-pilot, and just before he took off, he feathered one engine. He then took off with one engine, turned into the dead engine, and landed on one engine. Then Doolittle repeated the process, but with the opposite engine feathered. Next he took on a co-pilot and showed him how to do what he had just done. Moreover, he was able to loop the Marauder on one engine.

In *The Bait Bites Back*, William S. Phillips shows off the most famous B-26 Marauder in the European theater. *Flak Bait* was part of the 449th Bomb Squadron, 322nd Bomb Group, Ninth Air Force. By war's end, it had completed 202 missions—more than any other American bomber in the ETO. *Flak Bait* flew from June 1943 until VE-Day, May 8, 1945. Its forward fuselage now resides at the National Air and Space Museum in Washington, D.C. Phillips' painting illustrates the cigar shape of the bomber, which made it aerodynamically efficient and allowed it to carry as much tonnage as a B-17.

Ruhr Express

Royal Canadian Air Force

Robert Bailey

NOT ONLY DID THE ROYAL CANADIAN AIR FORCE FLY IN BOMBER COMMAND, CANADA also produced its own Lancasters. Canadian-built Lancasters were known as Lancaster Xs, which were a version of the Lancaster III. Packard built copies of Rolls Royce Merlin engines on license from Rolls Royce—these engines were known as Merlin-28s. The first Canadian Lancaster built by Victory Aircraft was the KB700. Mrs. C.G. Powers, the wife of the Canadian Minister of National Defence for Air, christened the plane *Ruhr Express*. The Royal Canadian Air Force (RCAF) took possession of the plane on August 6, 1943, and Group Captain Reg Lane, RCAF, flew it to England. Lane went on to command the 405th Squadron and to complete three tours in Bomber Command.

Robert Bailey portrays the dramatic return of the *Ruhr Express* from a mission with the 419th Squadron over Berlin on the night of November 22–23, 1943. With the left outboard engine out of operation, Pilot Officer H.A. Floren and crew pass over a German train station at less than a hundred feet (30m). Trains were the primary means of travel during the World War II because gasoline was rationed and automobile travel was discouraged. As in Bailey's *Night Crossing*, the train is a steam-powered locomotive, which belched black smoke, making it easy to spot from the air. At night the station would have been blacked out, but Bailey has taken some liberties to capture the drama of the moment.

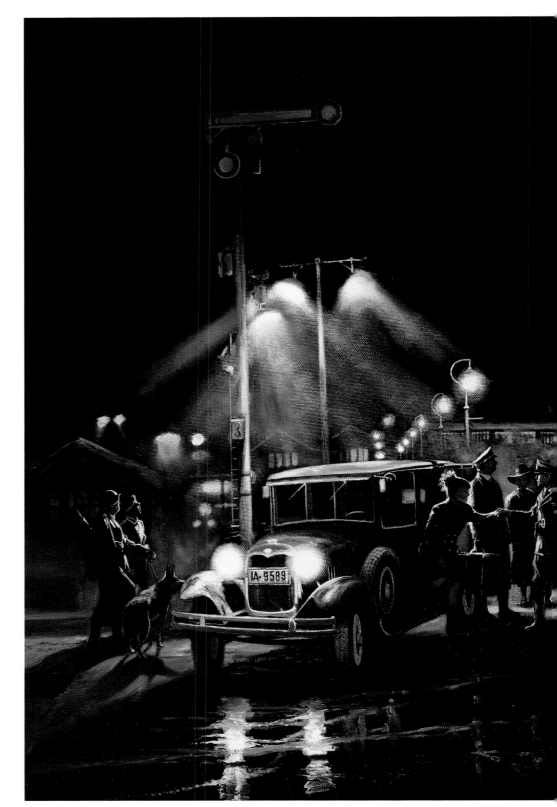

ROBERT BAILEY ©1998

Preparation

British Royal Air Force

Keith Woodcock

IN KEITH WOODCOCK'S *PREPARATION*, GROUND CREWS PREPARE A LANCASTER FOR A mission during the English winter. Men struggle with a tarpaulin while two others bring up scaffolding in order to service the Lancaster's Rolls Royce Merlin engines. A fuel bowser is seen to the front of the aircraft. A Lancaster with a 7,000-pound (3,175kg) bomb load could accommodate 2,580 Imperial gallons (11,729L), which is equal to 3,098 American gallons. The Lancaster's huge bomb bay allowed it to carry all manner of mines and bombs, including the two monstrosities designed by Dr. Barnes Wallis, the "Tallboy" and the "Grand Slam." The 12,000-pound (5,443kg) "Tallboy" revolved as it fell, increasing in speed until it broke the sound barrier. The "Grand Slam" was carried below the aircraft and weighed in at 22,000 pounds (9,979kg). Loading bombs was hard and potentially dangerous work. In May 1943 at Alconbury, a B-17 base of the 95th Bomb Group, several 500-pound (227kg) bombs exploded while being loaded, killing eighteen men, injuring twenty-one, and destroying four B-17s while damaging another eleven.

When bombers returned from missions, ground crews had the gruesome task of removing the wounded or dead and cleaning the blood, vomit, clothing, and body parts from the inside of the planes. Winter conditions in Lincolnshire, England, with the wind coming off the North Sea, made everything more difficult and time-consuming. Ground crews had to carry gear in bone-numbing cold. Base grounds would turn to mud and had to be covered by duckboards. The work of the ground crews was dirty and monotonous, but it had to be done carefully. Lives in the air depended on the performance of engines, pumps, oxygen systems, hydraulic systems, radios, and navigation systems. Crews painstakingly checked for any leaks in the fuel systems—fuel leaks were guaranteed catastrophes. Engines and parts had to be constantly repaired or replaced. Ground crews had to feed ammunition into belts for the aircraft's machine guns. Specialists might repair navigation and radio appliances, but most of the work was done by squadron mechanics, who often worked around the clock in preparation for a maximum effort.

An RAF bomber crew returns to base after a mission. From left to right are the observer, wireless operator, rear gunner, second pilot, and pilot captain.

Keith Woodcock

Max Effort

United States Army Air Force

Jim Dietz

JIM DIETZ SHOWS TWO B-24 BOMBER CREWS GATHERED AROUND *PAPER DOLL* IN HIS *Max Effort*. The jeep and the planes belong to the 449th Bomb Group stationed at Grottaglie, near Taranto in southern Italy. Visible through the jeep's windshield, an airman covers his face, evoking the emotional cost in dead comrades associated with a maximum effort, when all available planes and crews are mobilized to strike an important target. Standing in front of the right inboard engine, a crewmember points out damage to the engine nacelle to a ground crewman standing on the plane's wing.

The Fifteenth Air Force was established on November 1, 1943, by combining squadrons from the Twelfth and Ninth Air Forces. Under the command of Major General James "Jimmy" Doolittle and headquartered at Foggia, Italy, the Fifteenth Air Force gave flexibility to the American strategic bomber fleets. When weather in England closed down air bases, American B-17s and B-24s would, in theory, still be able to launch operations from Italy. The Fifteenth Air Force was also capable of hitting southern Germany, Austria, Hungary, Czechoslovakia, the Balkans, and Romania, most of which were beyond the range of the Eighth Air Force. Not all of the American bomber groups could squeeze into England, which was crowded with Bomber Command and Eighth Air Force fields as well as Fighter Command and Coastal Command. Fifteenth Air Force bombers hit oil targets in Vienna, Regensburg, and Ploesti, as well as the Messerschmitt aircraft factory at Wiener-Neustadt, Austria. The Fifteenth Air Force never captured the public imagination quite as thoroughly as the Eighth Air Force, in much the same manner as the B-24 has been overshadowed by the B-17. The Fifteenth Air Force flew many missions in support of Allied troops, especially at the Anzio beachhead from January to May 1944. The most controversial bombing episode of the Italian campaign occurred when heavy bombers destroyed the Benedictine abbey of Monte Cassino in February 1944.

Night Raiders

British Royal Air Force

Stan Stokes

BRITAIN'S AIR CHIEF MARSHAL SIR ARTHUR HARRIS PROCLAIMED: "WE CAN WRECK Berlin from end to end if the US Army Air Forces will come in to it. It will cost us four hundred to five hundred aircraft. It will cost Germany the war." Harris sent his bombers to Berlin from November 1943 to March 1944—the Americans did not "come into it." The average raid cost Bomber Command 5 percent; some raids cost as much as 9 percent of the bomber force. Bomber Command lost 1,128 bombers that winter over Berlin. Disastrous losses over Schweinfurt precluded the Eighth Air Force from making deep penetration raids without fighter escorts.

Thirty times larger than Hamburg, Berlin could not easily be burned down. While Hamburg was a medieval wooden city with many half-timbered houses and narrow streets, Berlin was a modern city built of stone, with broad avenues that acted as fire breaks. Berlin was also beyond the range of Oboe, the radio navigation apparatus, and the city was so big that it obscured H^{2}S radar, which depended on rivers and lakes to provide contrast to built-up urban areas. Berlin had too much built-up area for H^{2}S to function properly. The raid on Berlin was a defeat for Air Marshal Harris and Bomber Command. The single worst losses occurred over Nuremberg on the night of March 30–31, 1944, when ninety-five bombers out of 795 failed to return—a loss rate of 12 percent.

Welcome Home Yank
United States Army Air Force

William S. Phillips

THE B-24 LIBERATOR IS COMING HOME ON THREE ENGINES. THE RIGHT OUTBOARD engine is out and the left outboard engine is trailing smoke, most likely from an oil leak. The pilot and navigator have already made their calculations that the bomber can make it to some airfield on this compass heading. At this altitude, if the left engine seizes up, the pilot will have to put the plane into the Channel, and B-24s are not as friendly to ditch as B-17s. Where a B-17 would float long enough for its crew to exit, B-24 pilots often did not make it out in time. With the RAF Spitfire above him, at least the B-24's position would be known to air-sea rescue, but the Channel is cold at any time of year. The white cliffs of Dover beckon in the background, and the Liberator does not have much farther to go.

In 1943, the Spitfire was often employed in Channel patrols owing to its speed and firepower, but also because of its relatively short range. Designed in the mid-1930s to defend the British Isles, this 1943 Spitfire Mark IX had a range of a little more than 430 miles (692km). No matter its range, it appears as a guardian angel to this B-24 and Phillips' *Welcome Home Yank* looks back nostalgically at the Anglo-American alliance that won World War II.

Aries

United States Army Air Force

Roy Grinnell

FROM MAY TO JULY 1944, ALL TWELVE B-24S OF THE 834TH BOMB SQUADRON WERE painted with a different sign of the Zodiac by Sgt. Phil Brinkman. Together they were known as the Zodiac Squadron. Shown here is the aircraft flown by Captain Carl McCabe, bearing the sign of Aries, the ram. Roy Grinnell has rendered the plane in such vivid detail that it is possible to count the rivets. For most of the flight, the bombardier would man the B-24's front power turret, where it mounted two .50-caliber Browning machine guns. Behind the power turret is the astrodome through which the navigator could shoot the stars to double-check his location; the navigator's window appears just below and slightly aft of the astrodome. Just next to the word Aries is the pitot tube, which contained instruments for judging air speed. At the front of the plane is the bomb-aiming panel that gave the bombardier a vantage point as he lay on the bombardier's couch and lined up the target in the bombsight. Below the cockpit appear eight bombs, indicating that this plane has completed eight missions. Notice that the pilot's name and the bombs have been drawn on a symmetrical plate of exterior armor, which protected the co-pilot on the right side of the aircraft. Just aft of the pilot's compartment is the emergency escape hatch and next to that is the power dorsal turret and its twin .50-caliber machine guns.

To the right of *Aries* in formation is *Libra*. The "O" on *Libra's* tail and upper right wing surface denotes the group, in this case the 486th Bomb Group; the "C" is the plane's identification and the "2S" is the squadron code of the 834th. Also visible on *Libra* below the national insignia is the ball turret, which on the B-24 is retracted into the aircraft for landing because the tricycle landing gear of the B-24 did not afford the same ground clearance as that of the B-17.

Zodiac Double Trouble

United States Army Air Force

Roy Grinnell

IN *ZODIAC DOUBLE TROUBLE*, ROY GRINNELL DEPICTS *GEMINI*, WHICH WAS FLOWN BY Captian Andy Fuller. The dorsal turret gunner looks back towards the second Zodiac Squadron bomber next to it in formation. All three engine nacelles show signs of oil leaks, as witnessed by the dark smudges on the wings. On the top of the fuselage is a tear-shaped device known as the D/F Loop, a directional finding antenna. Behind the D/F Loop is the dorsal antenna.

The 486th Bomb Group and its bomb squadrons (832nd, 833rd, 834th, 835th) became operational in May 1944 and flew B-24s until mid-July 1944. Based in Sudbury in Suffolk, the 834th set an enviable record: it did not lose a single aircraft or crew member on its first one hundred missions. Owing to the different flight characteristics, the Eighth Air Force wanted to segregate the B-24s from the B-17s, allowing fighters to escort bombers that flew at the same speed and altitude. B-24s cruised with bomb loads at more than 220 miles per hour (354kph), about ten to fifteen miles an hour (16–24kph) faster than B-17s. But the B-17s flew several thousand feet higher than the B-24s. Therefore, the 486th had its B-24s replaced by B-17s. The famous Zodiac Squadron served as replacements for bomb squadrons in the Eighth Air Force's 3rd Division that continued to fly Liberators. The B-24 crews were skeptical about switching over to B-17s, but soon appreciated flying higher above the German flak, and the pilots admired the ease of handling of their new planes. The bombardiers and navigators appreciated the increased room in the nose of the B-17, and everyone preferred the heating system in the Flying Fortress.

Keith Woodcock

Safe

United States Army Air Force

Keith Woodcock

SNOW WAS THE ENEMY OF GROUND CREWS AND AIR CREWS ALIKE. THE WEATHER IN England was so fickle that American pilots claimed it could change from taxi to takeoff. Snow made assembling into formations an extremely hazardous business, increasing the risk of fully loaded bombers colliding with one another. Bomber groups employed forming ships, which were brightly painted retired bombers that dropped flares to aid the assembling of bomber formations. In the case of the 445th Bomb Group at Tibenham, which was east of Lowestoft and south of Norwich in Norfolk, the forming ship was painted in ten alternating orange and black strips.

In the winter of 1943–1944, the 445th Bomb Group was flying NOBALL missions. NOBALL was the code-name for attacks on V-weapon sites in the region of the Pas de Calais on the French coast. The Eighth Air Force dropped 1,700 tons (1542t) of high-explosive bombs on twenty-two of these targets over that winter.

Keith Woodcock's *Safe* illustrates the camaraderie of ground crews and aircrews, using the 445th Bomb Group, located in rural Norfolk, as his subject. When this B-24 landed, its left landing gear collapsed, causing it to lose its left outboard engine while spinning off the runway to the left. Dragging metal on concrete was an invitation to fire, which in a wounded bomber often resulted in a fatal explosion. Woodcock paints the ground crew rushing to save their comrades from potential catastrophe. This time the snow, always so dangerous in the air, has probably saved the bomber's crew from a more serious eventuality.

Fighting Their Way Out
United States Army Air Force

William S. Phillips

WILLIAM S. PHILLIPS ILLUSTRATES WHY THE CHIN TURRET WAS ADDED TO THE B-17. In order to cope with German head-on attacks, B-17G models with twin .50-caliber Browning M2 machine guns began arriving in the European theater in September 1943. *Fighting Their Way Out* demonstrates the German head-on attack as well as the massed firepower of the Flying Fortress in formation.

The Me 110 heavy fighter came up short against the RAF Spitfires and Hurricanes during the Battle of Britain, but it was the mainstay of the German night defense. Here two Me 110s dive headlong through the formation of the 381st Bomb Group. Normally the Me 110s stayed at some distance from the bomber formations because they were equipped with 30mm cannon that outranged the .50-caliber machine guns of the bombers, or they could fire 21cm rockets at the B-17s from a safe distance. The Me 110 in the foreground is equipped to carry rockets and the gunner may already have fired his.

The American .50-caliber machine gun had a rate of fire of some five hundred rounds per minute. Gunners were taught to fire in bursts because they would either jam their weapons or run out of ammunition if they held down their triggers for too long. Counting the chin turret and the ball turret on the B-17 at the upper right, the twin guns of the dorsal turret and the right waist gun of the Fortress in the foreground, there are seven .50-caliber guns firing at the diving Me 110. The closing speed of the planes would have been about 570 miles per hour (917kph), which would have exposed the Me 110 to 156 .50-caliber rounds in 2.7 seconds. The tracer rounds, which accounted for about every fourth round, were designed to let the gunners know where their rounds were going. Here, the tracer rounds are tracking into the lower right wing of the Me 110—the dorsal gunner and the right waist gunner of the Fortress in the center are scoring hits against the Me.

Tail-End Charlie

United States Army Air Force

Stan Stokes

STAN STOKES PICTURES ONE OF THE STRANGER INCIDENTS OF THE BOMBER CAMPAIGN on January 29, 1944, when a B-24 piloted by Captain E.W. Bruce of the 446th Bomb Group dueled with a Fw 190 at ground level over Liege, Belgium. For a mission against Frankfurt, Bruce's squadron, the 704th, drew low formation and Bruce's plane, the *Hula Wahine*, ended up flying tail-end Charlie. With all four of his superchargers out, Bruce had to sneak home at low altitude. Emerging from low clouds over Belgium, German fighters wounded three of the plane's gunners. Then the Fw 190, shown in the upper right, picked up the wounded plane. On the outskirts of Liege, Bruce narrowly missed the thatched roof of a

Belgian farmhouse. Because its tail guns were not working, the B-24 turned into the path of the German, leaving both planes on a collision course until the *Hula Wahine's* nose-turret bombardier shot down the 190.

Central to Stoke's snapshot is the prop wash of the plane, which blows thatch off the roof and the hat off the farmer's head. Laundry tears away from the line and chicken feathers fill the air. *Tail-End Charlie* offers us a rare glimpse of the underside of a big bomber. The gray camouflage is clearly delineated and the ball turret is safely retracted into the plane. Damage to the right wing and the left waist gunner's position is plainly visible.

Hans-Ulrich Rudel at Work

German Air Force

Keith Ferris

OBERSTLEUTNANT (LIEUTENANT COLONEL) HANS-ULRICH RUDEL MADE A LIVING FLYING the Ju 87 Stuka dive-bomber on the Russian front. Stuka was short for *Sturzkampfflugzeug*, a generic term for any dive-bomber. The Ju 87 was obsolete when the war began, but it gained fame from newsreel footage of its screaming dive-bomb attacks in Poland in 1939 and in France in 1940. It had to be withdrawn from the Battle of Britain because its top speed of less than 200 miles per hour (322kph) couldn't compete in the face of Hurricanes and Spitfires—it was like sending a lamb to the slaughter. The plane kept reinventing itself, and the Ju 87G-1 variant, armed with two 37mm cannon hung below the wing and outboard of each of the nonretractable legs, enjoyed a renaissance as the Nazis' best tank-killer on the Eastern Front.

Rudel did it better than any other dive-bomber pilot in the war. In fact his career symbolized the lack of any tour of duty for German pilots—they served until they died, were wounded, or were promoted to a desk job. According to his memoir, *Stuka Pilot*, the secret to tank-killing was being on a front that was in flux, where there was no dug-in antiaircraft artillery. Where antiaircraft guns were strongly emplaced, it was foolhardy to go tank-busting. Even an ace tank-buster like Rudel needed fighters to strafe gun positions. By diving from 600 feet (183m) and pulling out at less than fifty feet (15m), Rudel could hit the engine, ammunition, or fuel supply of a Soviet T-34, the Russian medium tank. Over the course of the war, Rudel is credited with having destroyed 519 Soviet tanks during 2,530 sorties in which he lost thirty Ju 87s.

In addition to the tank-killing, Rudel sank the battleship *Marat* off Leningrad, shot down eleven fighters, and destroyed thirteen locomotives, all in the Stuka.

In January 1945, Hitler awarded famed Stuka ace Hans-Ulrich Rudel the Golden Oak Leaves, Swords and Diamonds. Rudel was the sole recipient of this special award. Shown here, left to right, are Dieter Hrabak, Rudel, Walter Henschel (Rudel's tail gunner), and Adolf Hitler.

Maple Leaf Halifaxes

Royal Canadian Air Force

Robert Taylor

There could not have been an RAF in World War II without the contributions of the British Dominions. The RAF had 487 squadrons of which one hundred were from Canada, Australia, South Africa, India, or New Zealand. Of 340,000 aircrew in the RAF, some 134,000—nearly 40 percent— were from the Dominions. Thanks to the Ottawa Agreement of December 1939, Canada provided flight instruction to Canadians, Britons, Australians, and New Zealanders. By 1942 Canada was turning out some eleven thousand pilots and seventeen thousand aircrews per year.

THE FOUR-ENGINE HALIFAX WAS A RUGGED AND VERSATILE AIRCRAFT, BUT SOMEWHAT heavy-handed to fly compared with the other British bombers. The Halifax served throughout World War II as bomber, transport, ferry, air ambulance, paratroop carrier, and naval reconnaissance plane. Twice withdrawn from service due to heavy loss rates, the introduction of the Mark III type with rectangular fins, seen here, solved the problem of rudder stalls caused by the previous triangular fin design. Because it flew at lower altitudes than the Lancaster, the Halifax was at greater risk from German night fighters.

The plane depicted here was BB-B, *Bambi*, of 424 Squadron of the No. 6 Bomb Group, Royal Canadian Air Force (RCAF), flown by Flight Lieutenant Jack Dundas, DFC (Distinguished Flying Cross). Some 94,000 officers and men of the RCAF served overseas during World War II, with the majority serving in British groups within Bomber Command. Owing to the insistence of Charles Power, Canada's Minister of National Defense, Canadians formed their own all-volunteer squadrons. When conscription was introduced in November 1944, Powers resigned. By January 1943, eight Canadian bomber squadrons formed No. 6 Group, which lost more than a hundred bombers from March through June 1943. Morale suffered consequently, but picked up when Halifaxes and Lancasters replaced the obsolescent Wellingtons and the group received a new commander, Air Vice Marshal Clifford "Black Mike" McEwen. Throughout the bomber campaign, No. 6 Group dropped one-eighth of Bomber Command's bombs and lost 3,500 men killed. Another 4,700 Canadians died while serving in British squadrons.

Bomber Force

British Royal Air Force

Nicolas Trudgian

FOUR-ENGINE BOMBERS BEGAN TO REPLACE BRITAIN'S TWIN-ENGINE BOMBER FLEET IN 1942. As they did, the number of aircraft remained constant but the tonnage of dropped bombs increased by 44 percent. No bomber, not even the Boeing B-29 Superfortress, accounted for more tonnage than the Lancaster did, dropping more than 608,000 tons (551,568t). An outgrowth of the unsuccessful twin-engine Manchester, the Lancaster could carry the largest bombs of World War II: the 12,000 pound (5,443t) "Tallboy" and the 22,000 pound (9,979kg) "Grand Slam," the so-called blockbuster bomb.

The first squadrons equipped with the Lancaster were No. 44 Squadron and No. 97 Squadron at Woodhall Spa in Lincolnshire. No. 617 Squadron, the Dambusters, was also based at Woodhall and, following the death of Guy Gibson, was led by Wing Commander Leonard Cheshire, Victoria Cross. Under Cheshire's command No. 617 Squadron, shown here, engaged in several other famous precision raids. On the night of June 8–9, 1944, No. 617 Lancasters, reinforced by No. 88 Squadron, knocked out the bridge across the Loire River and the Saumur tunnel, blocking the movement of German troops from south-west France to Normandy. Later that year, on November 12, joined by No. 9 Squadron, No. 617 sank the German battleship *Tirpitz*, the 42,000-ton (38,102t) sister ship of the *Bismarck*, in the Trömso Fjord in Norway with two direct hits from the "Tallboys." As the *Tirpitz* went down her 1,200-man crew was heard singing "*Deutschland über alles.*"

Little Willie Coming Home

United States Army Air Force

Keith Ferris

ON MARCH 6, 1944, THE EIGHTH AIR FORCE BOMBED BERLIN. NEARLY NINE HUNDRED American bombers took part, including the B-17G named *Little Willie* from the 388th Bomb Group stationed in Knettishall, England. Over Berlin, flak knocked out two engines and sent *Little Willie* into a dive. Lt. Bernard M. Dopko, the pilot, struggled to regain control as the plane dove towards the suburbs of Berlin, pulling out below fifty feet (15m). Bombardier William Kelly warned, "Look out, Dop, you're going to run into the curb!" For the return flight over Germany, *Little Willie* flew below 100 feet (30m) at 115 miles per hour (185kph). At one point, Dopko had to bank the craft between two church spires because he could not fly over them. With its radio shot out, the bomber was unable to make contact for nine hours and was listed as missing in action. Finally, as *Little Willie* cruised ten feet (3m) over the English Channel, Dopko coaxed a third engine back to life long enough to climb to 5,000 feet (1,524m), high enough to reach Knettishall.

The Eighth Air Force lost sixty-nine bombers out of the 814 deployed in the raid on Berlin, along with eleven fighter aircraft out of the more than nine hundred that took part; seven hundred American airmen died that day. The German losses ran to less than fifty pilots killed or wounded, but after nine and one-half hours, Dopko landed *Little Willie* back at Knettishall. *Little Willie* had made it home.

One Down

United States Army Air Force

William S. Phillips

WHEN THE WAR BEGAN, EIGHTH AIR FORCE PLANES WERE PAINTED OLIVE DRAB ON upper surfaces and neutral gray on undersurfaces. Paint on surviving B-17s and B-24s darkened from exposure to the sun and the elements, becoming an almost purplish brown. Some bomb groups applied RAF camouflage using dark green and light brown on upper surfaces and pale blue gray on undersurfaces. Beginning in August 1942, a medium green was applied to all leading edges of the wings and to about 20 percent of the surface area of the tail. Camouflage painting was discontinued at the factories in January 1944 because it saved on the man-hours involved in applying two different colors to each plane, thus increasing production. Unpainted planes flew slightly faster owing to the decrease in weight and drag. Propellers were painted a dull black except for the yellow four-inch propeller tip. The leading surface in front of the pilot and co-pilot was also covered in flat black to prevent glare.

The first bombers to arrive unpainted were B-17Gs, like the plane seen in *One Down*. This plane has just finished its first mission and appears without the identifying nose art or squadron markings. The aluminum skin of the B-17G gleams in the sunlight and displays rows of interlocking rivets. The chin turret of the G model shows off the twin .50-caliber machine guns that upgraded the frontal protection of the B-17 to that of the B-24. Initially, bomber crews were naturally reluctant to fly in unpainted aircraft, thinking that enemy fighters would single them out because of their increased visibility. Commanders attempted to integrate unpainted, silver planes into their squadrons when possible until all the aircraft in a group were silver, but camouflaged aircraft continued to arrive from depots through June 1944, and squadrons flew camouflaged craft until the end of the war.

Milk Run

United States Army Air Force

Nixon Galloway

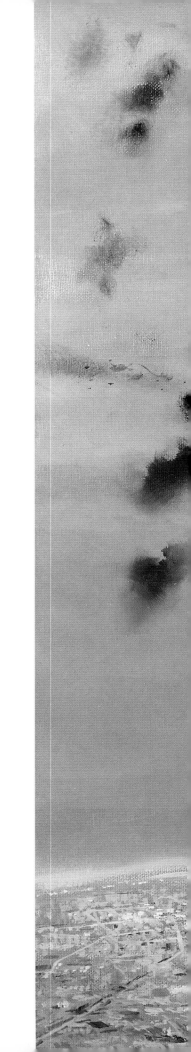

On March 19, 1944, 172 heavy bombers of the Eighth Air Force attacked German V-1 weapon installations on the French coast. V-weapons were the *Vergeltungswaffen*, or vengeance weapons, designed to punish Britain for bombing Germany. The V-1 was the first cruise missile, but its 125-mile (201km) range limited its deployment to the French and Dutch coasts if it was to be able to hit southern England. Flight Officer Constance Babington Smith, photo reconnaissance officer, first located missile sites at Peenemünde on the Baltic coast in November 1943, but the head of scientific intelligence, R.V. Jones, had ordered the photo reconnaissance mission based on reports from secret agents in occupied Europe.

The mission of the 100th Bomb Group's 350th Bomb Squadron was to attack the V-1 missile site near Boulogne in the Pas de Calais. A "milk run" was a mission that was close to home and not very dangerous. Unfortunately for the B-17G *Miss Irish* flown by Captain John Gibbons, an .88mm flak round struck the plane behind the right wing, blasting away the radio compartment and the radio operator. Missions over occupied France were in danger primarily from antiaircraft weapons such as artillery and rockets; rocket contrails can be seen in the right foreground. Amazingly, the plane was held together by the upper and left sides of the fuselage, but the explosion destroyed the crew's parachutes, which made bailing out impossible. Gibbons nursed the aircraft back to England, landing at the first airfield that presented itself, a P-47 fighter base at Raydon near Ipswich. Using the entire runway for his landing, Gibbons let *Miss Irish* coast to a halt because he feared that braking the craft would break it in two. The aircraft was a complete write-off and was salvaged for parts.

No Empty Bunks Tonight
United States Army Airforce

William S. Phillips

NO AIRCREW WANTED TO BE THE LAST PLANE IN A BOMBER FORMATION BECAUSE THE last plane was vulnerable to German fighter attack and used more gasoline flying in the wake of turbulence of all the forward aircraft. Last planes were referred to as "tail-end Charlies" and were often never seen again. Pilots and crews tried to avoid that assignment the same way squadrons wanted to avoid being the lowest squadron of the three in a group. The B-24 in this hypothetical drama is about to make it back to its base in East Anglia, and to return its crew to their bunks. Empty bunks in bomb squadrons, like empty seats in the mess hall, had a devastating impact on the morale of the surviving bomber crews.

The B-24J appeared in April 1944 armed with a power turret in the nose, which was designed to cope with the German head-on fighter attacks that had begun the previous autumn. The power turret, however, added weight to the B-24 and seriously impacted its already cumbersome handling characteristics by making the plane even more nose-heavy. Moreover, it diminished the space in the nose of the aircraft, making it even more difficult for the navigator and the bombardier to carry out their jobs. The turret also diminished the bomb-carrying capacity of the B-24, denying it one of the main advantages that it held over the B-17. Because of the power turret, the B-24 had to fly lower than the B-17, which exposed it to more accurate German flak and a greater number of German fighters.

B-24 pilots coped with the awkward characteristics of the Liberator by climbing high and then descending to the cruising altitude, which allowed them to cruise with the plane's bulbous nose at a slightly downward angle, thereby increasing visibility. To merely climb to cruising altitude left the pilot fighting to see out of the front of the plane and increased the risk of collision in formation.

Clash Over Haseleunne

United States Army Air Force

Robert Bailey

On March 6, 1944, Lt. General James H. Doolittle sent more than seven hundred bombers of the Eighth Air Force against Berlin, all three air divisions in the following order: 1st, 3rd, 2nd. Fighters did not continuously escort the bombers; rather, they provided umbrella coverage at certain points on the way to the target. The fighters that were to protect the 3rd Air Division took off late, and a navigational error increased the planned gap between two bomber wings from twelve to twenty miles (19km to 32km). Subsequently, German fighters fell on the exposed 100th Bomb Group's 351st Bomb Squadron like hungry sharks.

Robert Bailey puts us at 21,000 feet (6401km) over Haseleunne, about twenty miles (32km) from the Dutch border where Oldenburg meets Hanover. German single-engine aircraft are fighting with P-47 Thunderbolts to deny the bombers their fighter cover. The P-47 here is from the 56th Fighter Group, 61st Fighter Squadron, as evidenced by the HV on the fuselage and the white nose cowling. Majors Francis S. Gabreski and Robert S. Johnson of the 61st Fighter Squadron were the top-scoring aces in the Eighth Air Force, each having shot down twenty-eight planes. But even the best fighter squadron in the Eighth Air Force could not win the battle that day, and the Germans destroyed virtually the entire 351st Bomb Squadron, shooting down fifteen planes. In *Clash Over Haseleunne* the battle swirls around *Our Gal Sal*, piloted by Lieutenant Robert Shoens. When Shoens touched down hours later at Thorpe Abbots in Norfolk, he was the sole bomber to do so—the only one of four from his squadron to return. The Eighth Air Force lost sixty-nine bombers and eleven fighters, making March 6, 1944, the most costly day in the history of the bombing campaign.

Lt. Owen D. "Cowboy" Roane, legendary pilot of the 100th Bomb Group, led a number of tough missions, including the raids on Regensburg and Schweinfurt.

No Trains Today

United States Army Air Force

Stan Stokes

THIS DOUGLAS A-20 HAVOC LIGHT BOMBER HAS JUST BLOWN UP A GERMAN AMMUNITION train. A superb ground-attack aircraft, the A-20 had been through several reincarnations during the war and was still giving useful service in 1944. Prior to the Allied invasion of Normandy, General Dwight D. Eisenhower, the supreme Allied commander, demanded operational control of the strategic air forces. Air Chief Marshal Sir Arthur Harris, commander of Bomber Command, and Lt. General Carl A. Spaatz, commander of United States strategic air forces, objected strenuously to the loss of operational independence. Eisenhower wanted the strategic air forces to destroy the French railway system leading from Paris to the likely invasion beaches in the Pas de Calais and Normandy. When the bomber generals protested that bombing railroad marshalling yards would kill too many French civilians, Prime Minister Churchill agreed with Harris and Spaatz. Eisenhower had to threaten to resign before Churchill relented, and on April 14, 1944, the Combined Chiefs of Staff authorized Eisenhower to command the strategic air forces in what was called the Transportation Plan.

As it turned out, the strategic air forces performed yeoman's service destroying the French railroad system, but the fighter-bombers and the light bombers, such as the Douglas A-20 Havoc, were even more accurate. Bombing and strafing from low altitude was hazardous, and this A-20 is lucky to have escaped being blown up along with the train. No pilot would dare to fly directly over a train while strafing it, for obvious reasons. By the end of the war, planes such as the A-20s and P-47s had essentially wiped out the steam-powered, coal-burning locomotives seen here in Stan Stokes' *No Trains Today*.

Portrait of a Queen
United States Army Air Force

Stan Stokes

STAN STOKES BRINGS THE ROMANCE OF THE B-17G TO LIFE IN *PORTRAIT OF A QUEEN*. His romanticized portrait of this beauty makes it easy to see why B-17 crews were so partial to the Flying Fortress. Rugged and durable, the aircraft was also smooth to fly and beautiful to behold. Although it could not fly as fast or as far as the B-24, and even though its bomb load was smaller, the B-17 captured the attention and the imagination of the World War II generation.

The B-17 bombardier manned the guns when he was not aiming the bombs. If this plane belonged to the lead bombardier of a squadron it would contain the famous Norden bombsight, which automatically calculated the speed and course of the plane relative to the target and indicated whether the target was standing still or moving. In a raid, only the lead bombardier had a Norden bombsight and all the other planes dropped when the lead aircraft did. This put the bombs down on the target simultaneously, which sacrificed some accuracy for speed over the target. The nose of the Flying Fortress was larger than that of the Liberator and was appreciated by crews that had experience in both aircraft. The B-17G still retained its cheek guns on either side of the nose. Both the top and ball turrets contained twin .50-caliber machine guns; the twin guns of the lower B-17 are visible here as well.

These Flying Fortresses are from the 401st Bomb Group, as denoted by the white S in the black triangle on the plane's tail. The black SC on the fuselage indicates that they are in the 612th Bomb Squadron. Also on the tail is each aircraft's individual letter marking in black on the yellow strip. These planes took on this paint scheme in August 1944, and before the month was out would have bombed the German V-2 ballistic missile site at Peenemünde, Germany. The squadron was based at Deenethorpe, some sixty miles (97km) northwest of London.

A Test of Courage

United States Army Air Force

Keith Ferris

On August 15, 1944, the Eighth Air Force sent up more than 850 heavy bombers to strike airfields in Germany, Holland, and Belgium. The 303rd Bomb Group's 358th Bomb Squadron was flying low formation towards Wiesbaden when it was jumped by Focke Wulf 190s of the II JG (*Jadgeschwader* or Fighter Wing) 300 over Trier. Within minutes, II JG 300 had shot down nine Flying Fortresses. Shown here is the FW 190 flown by Klaus Bretschneider.

The Fw 190's two 20mm cannon and two 7.9mm machine guns are shredding the right wing of the Flying Fortress at the lower left; even self-sealing gas tanks could not withstand multiple cannon rounds containing tracer ammunition. Normally, the tail gunner would have begun firing at a thousand meters to frighten the German pilot with tracers. The tail turret gunner is visible, yet his guns are not bearing on the German. Most likely he is mortally wounded. *Luftwaffe* Major Werner Schroer, who was credited with 114 victories, told his young pilots to close their eyes when attacking from behind.

The tail gunner of a B-17 cleans his glass windshield before a mission. Lives depended on good vision and who saw whom first. The twin .50-caliber machine guns were an addition to the B-17E model, and Boeing engineers created an entirely new tail for the plane. Notice the ball and ring sight. This close-up look at an electrically heated flying suit reveals the heating elements, which resemble those of an electric blanket.

Ferris' *A Test of Courage* illustrates the terror of close combat in the air, and the bravery needed to carry it out. As Schroer told the producers of the Thames television documentary *The World at War*, "I was so close that I could really see the rear gunner, and I could see he was as frightened as I was."

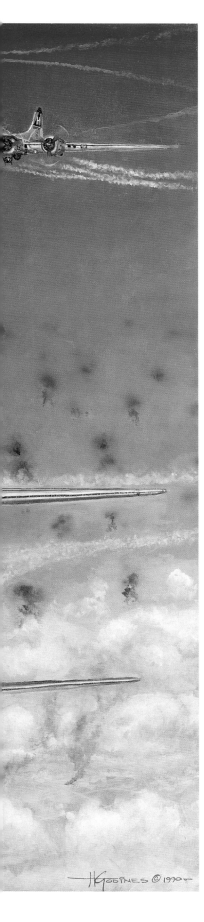

No Milkrun Today

United States Army Air Force

Henry Godines

At the start of their tour, six officers and four enlisted men pose in front of their B-17G, *Sweet Pea*, which was named after the baby in the Popeye cartoon. These men are members of the 303rd Bomb Group, one of the first American heavy bombardment groups to deploy to England. In 1942 two-thirds of their predecessors did not complete their combat tours. In the nose of the plane, the super-secret Norden bombsight is covered with a canvas bag.

MILKRUN SPECIAL, FLOWN BY COLONEL JOHN A. MURPHY, leads the 306th Bomb Group against a synthetic oil plant at Ruhland on October 7, 1944. By October 1944, Germany had thirty thousand flak guns. Though the Germans had to expend about sixteen thousand shells for every bomber they knocked down, in 1944 flak destroyed 3,500 American planes, some six hundred more than German fighters destroyed. Here the flak appears as ugly black bursts in the background.

On this raid, the 306th experienced an attack by Me 262s from Brandenburg. But the reputation of the vaunted German jet was essentially unfounded. The German rocket plane, the Me 163 *Komet*, was far more of a threat to the bombers. Forty-three German pilots shot down Allied aircraft while flying Me 262s and twenty-two of them became jet aces by shooting down five or more planes. Fewer than a hundred bombers were lost to Me 262s. While the Me 262 was heavily armed with four 30mm cannon, the closing speed of the bombers and the Me 262 was 800 miles per hour (1,287kph), too fast for accurate shooting. Therefore, German jet pilots preferred to dive on the bombers from five thousand feet (1,524m) above and pull up fifteen hundred feet (457m) below and forty-five hundred feet (1372m) behind the bomber stream. Then, with their cannon converging at 1,200 feet (366m) in front of them, the Me 262s would hunt for bombers.

Schweinfurt Again
United States Army Air Force

Keith Ferris

FOR SOME PLANES THE LAW OF AVERAGES SEEM NOT TO APPLY. HERE, KEITH FERRIS commemorates the eightieth mission of *Thunder Bird* against Schweinfurt on October 9, 1944. For the 303rd Bomb Group from Molesworth, England, this was the fifth time they had flown this mission and it was the second trip to Schweinfurt for *Thunder Bird*. The painted bombs marking the missions, every fifth bomb in white, stretch from the cheek gun of the navigator back past the cockpit and stop even with the dorsal turret. The Eighth Air Force retired this bomber in March 1945 following its 116th mission. The plane has been around so long that it still wears camouflage paint.

By this time in the war the numerical superiority of the Anglo-American bomber fleets was becoming readily apparent. Bomber Command had a thousand four-engine bombers. The Eighth Air Force had two thousand with two crews per bomber, while the Fifteenth Air Force had twelve hundred four-engine bombers with two crews. From June to October 1944 the German Air Force was losing twenty-six hundred pilots each month.

Albert Speer, Hitler's minister of armaments, said after the war that the Allies could have ended the war earlier if they had stuck to bombing armaments in 1943 instead of engaging in what he called "pointless area bombing." Following the first Schweinfurt raid in August 1943 ball-bearing production fell by thirty-eight percent; but Germany had four other ball-bearing plants and output soon increased beyond the preattack figures. The second attack in October 1943 caused a 67 percent drop in ball-bearing production, but the Germans substituted slide bearings, and the Allies did not gain much from their success. The third round of attacks in February 1944 caused ball-bearing production to fall by 29 percent to what it was in December 1943, but in April 1944 the raids stopped as focus was shifted to the implementation of the Transportation Plan. "Thus," Speer wrote in his memoirs, *Inside the Third Reich*, "the Allies threw away success when it was already in their hands."

Under Attack

United States Army Air Force

Roy Grinnell

FEW BOMB GROUPS WERE AS VISUALLY STRIKING AS THE 459ᵀᴴ BOMB GROUP OF THE Fifteenth Air Force in Italy. With its yellow and black checkerboard tail fins and black diamonds on its tail, yellow engine cowlings, black leading edge de-icing boots, and black anti-glare panel, the B-24 is clearly the star of this painting and the Focke Wulf 190s are merely incidental. Piloted by Lieutenant Carl L. McKinnon, Jr., the B-24 flies above the clouds of the southern Alps; yellow bombs on the red background below the cockpit show that this plane has flown twenty-three missions.

Fifteenth Air Force crews had to fly a tour of fifty missions, but they received double tour credits for long and difficult missions over the Alps, such as the raids on the Messerschmitt complex at Wiener-Neustadt, or on Munich, or for missions to Ploesti in Romania. Flying over fourteen thousand–foot (4,267m) Alpine peaks was especially harrowing in a crippled bomber because there were so few safe places to crash land. To make things worse, neutral Switzerland would fire on bombers that encroached upon its airspace. When a bomber did put down in Switzerland, the American air attaché would examine the plane, and if he deemed it airworthy the crew was in serious trouble. Moreover, internment in Switzerland often meant being housed in unheated mountain hotels and fed a diet of potato soup: a fate that many American aviators went to great lengths to escape.

McKinnon's bomber, *Tall, Torrid and Texas*, features a bathing beauty wearing a red bathing suit and high heels. Nose art personified individual aircraft and often featured a shapely, scantily-clad woman to accompany the flashy name of the plane. Much nose art was derivative of the Vargas pinups that appeared in *Esquire* magazine during the war. The women are tall, leggy, and voluptuous. James Jones noted in his *WWII*, "when the presence of death and extinction are always around the corner, the comfort of women takes on great importance."

Alone No More

United States Army Air Force

William S. Phillips

SEEN HERE RETURNING HOME WITH ONE ENGINE OUT IS THE B-17G NAMED *Sweet Rose O'Grady* of the 303rd Bomb Group. *Sweet Rose* belonged to the 427th Bomb Squadron as indicated by the GN on the fuselage and the 4 at the top of the Triangle C. Having completed 124 missions, the plane was renowned. Aircraft became famous as they finished fifty, seventy-five, and a hundred missions, after which the Eighth Air Force often retired them for morale purposes.

Flying on three engines meant less altitude, which in turn put the bomber at risk from German fighters. But *Sweet Rose* has gotten friendly interception by two Spitfire Mk. IXs from the No. 261 Squadron. The Spitfire Mk. IX had been up-gunned to compete with Fw 190s and now mounted two 20mm cannon as well as machine guns. Also equipped with a more powerful Rolls-Royce Merlin engine, the Mark IX could fly cover over France to pick up returning bombers like *Sweet Rose*.

Sweet Rose has her right outboard propeller feathered. When pilots needed to shut down an engine, they had to turn the airscrew so that the blade of the propeller did not windmill. Windmilling meant that the propeller continued to revolve, which caused unsafe vibration that made the plane unstable and difficult to control. With a propeller in a feathered position, the biting edge of the blades turned into the wind, allowing the air to pass over each edge of the propeller equally, allowing it to remain stable through the air.

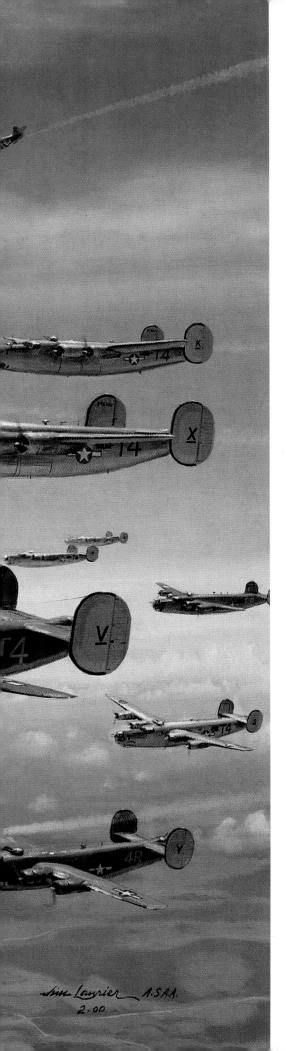

R-Bar Over Bielefeld

United States Army Air Force

Jim Laurier

ON NOVEMBER 2, 1944, THE EIGHTH AIR FORCE PUT UP MORE THAN ELEVEN HUNDRED heavy bombers to attack synthetic oil and transportation targets. The B-24s of the 489th Bomb Group bombed the railroad marshaling yards at Bielefeld, Germany, about equidistant between Hamm and Hanover. These bombers, bearing a large "T4" aft of the left waist gunner's position, are from the 847th Bomb Squadron. Jim Laurier's *R-Bar Over Bielefeld* marks the first large scale encounter with Kommando Nowotny, the first unit composed entirely of jet fighters. The Me 262 twin-engine jet fighters of Kommando Nowotny were led by twenty-three year old Major Walter Nowotny, one of Germany's most experienced and highly decorated fighter aces. The bomb squadrons of the 489th had heard rumors about the German jets but had never seen them until November 2.

As the *R-Bar* flies high formation away from the target, contrails appear in the sky above the squadron. Laurier depicts the first and only pass made by the German jets as they dove head on with dizzying speed through the twelve B-24s of the 847th. The Germans and the bombers were closing at such a high rate of speed, nearly 800 miles per hour (1,287kph), that neither side could hit the other even though the bombers' chin and dorsal turrets are clearly firing. Armed with four 30mm cannon but no machine guns, the Me 262 pilots hit nothing, and soon adopted stern attacks. Luckily for the American bombers, the escorting P-47s chased off the Me 262s, which did not return.

By this time in the war, the Eighth Air Force had so many bombers that squadrons like the 847th had to add a bar under the aircraft's identifying letter on the tail fin. In the case of *R-Bar* that meant there was another aircraft with an "R" on its tail fin. The Eighth Air Force lost forty heavy bombers that day but no bombers were lost from the 489th. Even the bomber with the smoking engine in the lower right foreground made it home.

A Welcome at the Inn

United States Army Air Force

Nicolas Trudgian

NICOLAS TRUDGIAN RECREATES THE RETURN OF HEAVY BOMBERS ON CHRISTMAS EVE, 1944. They have just attacked marshaling yards and concentration points behind the Belgian Ardennes where the Germans had begun their famous counterattack on December 16th. Bad weather had protected Hitler's final offensive until December 23. As a young boy and an airman watch from the front of "The Rose and Crown," a B-17 lines up its final approach on three-engines and behind it another Flying Fortress turns to follow. Across the river another B-17 banks to begin its landing at a different airfield, and high in the left background a squadron of B-17s heads for its base. An American truck and jeep are the only vehicles on the road and the chalkboard in the lower left announces, "Christmas Eve Party Tonight, USAAF Welcome!"

David Reynolds, Cambridge historian and authority on the American experience in Britain during the war, concludes that the air war brought American airmen and British civilians closer together. Some bomb squadrons had been stationed in East Anglia for more than two years; the 306th spent thirty-eight months in Thurleigh in Bedfordshire. Under those conditions, American airmen became regulars at nearby inns and were missed when their bombers failed to return.

Ironically, the First United States Army had requested that the Eighth Air Force bomb many of the German troop concentrations and assembly areas in Germany just two weeks earlier. Because the bomber generals eschewed such tactical use of bombers they denied the request, stating that the targets were not "remunerative."

Ruby's Fortress

United States Army Air Force

Stan Stokes

FOUR .50-CALIBER MACHINE GUNS BLAZE AWAY AT A BURNING FW 190. THE GERMAN plane has just made a head-on attack on *Ruby's Raiders*, a B-17G from the 385th Bomb Squadron at Great Ashfield in Suffolk. When Pfc. Ruby Newell, Women's Army Corps (WAC), was named the most attractive WAC in the ETO in 1944, the 385th painted this B-17 in her honor. Stan Stokes portrays perhaps the only bomber in the theater where the female subject was not only clothed, but in uniform.

The bombardier and copilot can be seen wearing their flying helmets, goggles, and oxygen masks for high-altitude flying. When walking around in the unpressurized plane, crewmen had to carry oxygen bottles or risk suffering from anoxia, an oxygen deficiency that could cause permanent damage or even death. Oxygen masks went on at twelve thousand feet (3,658m) and oxygen checks occurred every two thousand to three thousand feet (610m to 914m), beginning at fifteen thousand feet (4,572m) and continuing until cruising altitude was reached. Crewmen flying at high altitudes also had to make sure that their frozen breath did not clog the apparatus and prevent delivery of oxygen.

Bridge at Remagen, Arado 234

German Air Force

Keith Woodcock

ON MARCH 7, 1945, THE FIRST US ARMY CAPTURED INTACT THE LUDENDORFF RAILROAD bridge over the Rhine River at Remagen, ten miles (16km) south of Bonn. A week after the loss of the bridge, the KG 76 (*Kampfgeschwader* or Bomber Wing 76) sent its *Stabstaffel* (Headquarters flight) of twenty-one Arados to destroy it. By March 15, the Remagen bridge was the most heavily defended location in the European theater with two antiaircraft battalions guarding both banks of the Rhine. American gunners shot down fifteen of the jets at no cost to the bridge.

Able to fly at 460 miles per hour (740kph) with a 3,000-pound (1,361kg) bomb load, the plane came equipped with an ejection seat and a drogue parachute for landings. As the world's first operational jet bomber, the Arado Ar 234 deserves a footnote in aviation history, but it was more interesting than significant. Only about two hundred of the planes were produced after passing through eight variations in four years. The Mosquito could fly almost as fast as the Arado, and Britain and her dominions produced more than 5,500 of them.

~ Robert Taylor ~ 94 ~

Escort for the Straggler
Royal Air Force

Robert Taylor

Four Mk. IX Spitfires fly cover for a famous Lancaster that has survived another mission. Robert Taylor depicts a mission in the lengthy career of UL-M2 of the No. 576 Squadron out of Elsham Woods, Lincolnshire. The plane is making it back from a raid on the Reich with part of its left tail fin shot away. The accompanying Spitfires are out to make sure that no Me 410s sneaks in behind the bomber stream to take advantage of an unwary Lancaster. Although there were a number of Lancasters that racked up a hundred missions, M□, or *Mike Squared*, completed 140: ninety-eight over Germany and fifteen to Berlin. The Royal Air Force retired the four-engine bomber after its last mission in January 1944.

While the Germans were impressed by the Americans' flying in tight patterns and the speed with which their bombs fell from their formations, the British bombers carried much larger and more damaging ordnance. The British developed a 4,000-pound (1814kg) bomb with a light casing, which developed a pressure wave over a very large area. The explosive force created a vacuum. First the pressure wave blew out and then it collapsed, creating a suction effect. German women in deep shelters lived through repeated examples of this contraction of the pressure wave, which pulled their hair straight up on their heads.

No. 576 Squadron took part in the attacks on Berlin in the winter of 1943–1944, losing seven Lancasters in the first month of the campaign. In April 1944 the squadron took part in raids on V-weapon sites in France as well as attacks in Normandy and the Pas de Calais against transportation targets. *Mike Squared* bowed out in the winter of 1944–1945 while the squadron was attacking the German synthetic oil industry. In April 1945, the Lancasters of No. 576 Squadron made one last attack—on Hitler's Bavarian mountain retreat at Berchtesgaden.

Haruki Iki, Repulse and the Prince of Wales

Japanese Air Force

Keith Ferris

ON DECEMBER 10, 1940, JAPANESE MITSUBISHI G4MI (BETTY) BOMBERS BASED NEAR Saigon sank the *Repulse* and the *Prince of Wales* off the coast of Malaya. The medium bomber had tremendous range, more than 2,200 miles (3,540km), but it came at the expense of armor, armament, and self-sealing gas tanks. The Japanese called the plane the "Flying Cigar" on account of its shape, but American pilots called it the "Flying Zippo" because of its propensity to go up in flames.

Expecting a Japanese invasion, Vice Admiral Tom Phillips put to sea aboard the *Prince of Wales* with Task Force Z (*Repulse, Prince of Wales*, and several destroyers), intending to shoot up the Japanese force. Based upon submarine sightings, Japanese air groups took off from bases near Saigon to find Force Z. Shortly after 11:00 A.M., the 3rd Squadron of the Kanoya Air Group under Lieutenant Haruki Iki found the *Repulse*, but his Long Lance torpedo hung up and failed to drop. In the time it took Iki to go around, two other air groups had torpedoed the *Repulse*, as did Iki on his second pass. Hit by fourteen torpedoes, the cruiser sank at 12:33 P.M.; the battleship sank at 1:20 P.M. after being hit by seven torpedoes and three bombs.

The aircraft carrier *Indomitable* was unable to accompany the two capital ships as scheduled because she was in dry dock, but Prime Minister Churchill sent the ships anyway. Force Z set out from Singapore under Phillips, who believed that big ships need not fear attacks from aircraft. Following a heated argument with an RAF officer in the 1930s, the airman, well aware of the destructive potential of aerial attacks, predicted that one day Phillips would go down with his ship. Though this prediction came true, Phillips denied the significance of bombers to the very end. As his ship, the *Prince of Wales*, was being torpedoed and bombed, Phillips would say, "That was a great _____ mine."

In Alis Vincimus

United States Army Air Force

Gil Cohen

WEST OF THE INTERNATIONAL DATE LINE, IT WAS DECEMBER 8, 1941, WHEN JAPAN struck Clark Field in the Philippines without a declaration of war. Japanese naval bombers based on Formosa destroyed seventeen B-17s of the 19th Bomb Group on the ground, nearly nine hours after General Douglas MacArthur and his staff learned about Pearl Harbor.

Gil Cohen puts Captain Colin P. Kelly, Jr., at the center of the action in *In Alis Vincimus* (On Wings We Conquer). Kelly's plane had survived December 8th because it was based at Del Monte on the island of Mindanao. On December 10, the Mindanao B-17s of the 14th Bomb Squadron took on bombs adjacent to Clark Field, which is still burning in the background. Cohen captures the loading of bombs onto the B-17C at the onset of an air raid alert as the ground crews scramble to get the plane out of there. The bombs are visible under the bomb bay and the left inboard engine. Behind the right wheel of the aircraft is the ventral gun position, which resembled a bathtub and had two guns to protect the underside of the plane. The B-17C had no tail gun—a deficit that Japanese fighters would exploit fully. Neither was there a dorsal turret on this early model; only a single .50-caliber gun manned by the radio operator where the humpback met the fuselage.

With only three bombs, Kelly flew north to Aparri to bomb the landing fleet. There, he made good use of his limited payload, leaving one ship in flames. While returning to Clark Field, though, disaster struck. His bomber was attacked from the rear by Sergeant Saburo Sakai, one of Japan's greatest aces. Kelly fishtailed his plane to give his waist gunners a shot, but the gas tanks in the early B-17 were not self-sealing and finally succumbed to Sakai's withering fire. His plane on fire, Kelly dove for the safety of Clark Field. One man was already dead, but Kelly's courageous piloting of the doomed bomber allowed five men to successfully bail out. Although he died in the plane's explosion, Kelly would posthumously receive the Distinguished Service Cross. America had its first war hero.

Bottom of the First

United States Army Air Force

Jim Dietz

FOLLOWING THE IMPERIAL ARMY'S LUZON LANDINGS, THE JAPANESE INCREASED BOMBING runs on all the island's airfields. By December 13, 1941, they were operating fighters out of bases in the north and west of the island. This left vulnerable the remaining fourteen B-17s at Del Monte Airfield—a full 600 miles (965km) south on the island of Mindanao. Faced with Japanese command of the air, Major General Lewis Brereton reluctantly requested permission to fly his heavy bombers to Darwin, Australia, where they could be safely maintained.

In *Bottom of the First*, Jim Dietz depicts the scene on December 15th when B-17 crews began packing up to evacuate Del Monte. Though the Japanese had not yet discovered the bombers, time was of the essence. The body language of the pilot in the left foreground indicates he is receiving some unsettling news, and even the crew's English setter, alert at the rear of the vehicle, patiently awaits his orders. Thick wooden boxes filled with rations or ammunition litter the area, waiting to be loaded. In the right foreground, one of the ubiquitous 55-gallon (208L) oil drums rests next to the trunk of a tree. In the background, another Flying Fortress taxis into position, while a third rests under a camouflage net.

A lack of meaningful infrastructure in the Philippines was another compelling reason for moving operations to Australia. The bases had been primitive, lacking proper drainage, revetments, and radar. Without critical spare parts, such as engines and propellers, damaged bombers could not be properly rebuilt; parts had to be cannibalized from other aircraft. In fact, one Boeing B-17D that left for Australia was named after a line in a popular American song of the day: "Here comes little Alexander, what a funny looking gander; he's half swan and he's half goose, ha-ha-ha, he's just a Swoose." The plane's pilot, Captain Weldon Smith, thought Swoose was an appropriate name for a plane cobbled together from spare parts. Its lineage notwithstanding, the *Swoose* went on to become the command plane of Lieutenant General George Brett of the Far East Air Force. Among its notable passengers was Lieutenant Commander Lyndon B. Johnson, a future president of the United States.

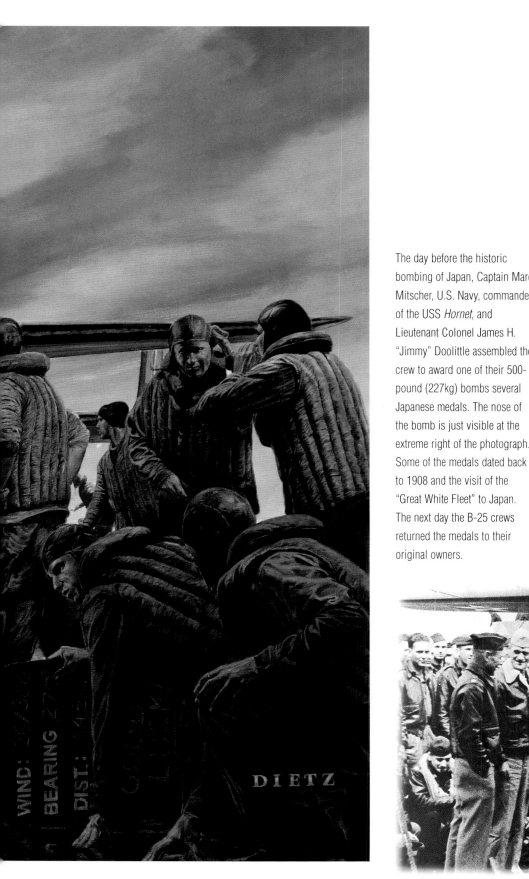

Early Launch

United States Army Air Force

Jim Dietz

The day before the historic bombing of Japan, Captain Marc Mitscher, U.S. Navy, commander of the USS *Hornet*, and Lieutenant Colonel James H. "Jimmy" Doolittle assembled the crew to award one of their 500-pound (227kg) bombs several Japanese medals. The nose of the bomb is just visible at the extreme right of the photograph. Some of the medals dated back to 1908 and the visit of the "Great White Fleet" to Japan. The next day the B-25 crews returned the medals to their original owners.

On April 19, 1942, an improbable exercise in aeronautical revenge was about to take place. To raise American morale, President Roosevelt had insisted his military exact payback for Pearl Harbor, and here, sixteen North American B-25 Mitchell bombers stand poised for a bombing mission targeting Japanese soil. With his airmen taking off from the carrier USS *Hornet*, naval flight instructor Lieutenant Henry Milller expected no problems. The B-25s had the wingspan and power required for the short take-off, and Miller had taught the army pilots what all naval aviators learned—how to take off with only 500 feet (152m) of runway. The mission, commanded by famed aviator Lieutenant Colonel James Doolittle, would launch a full 500 miles (805km) from the Japanese coast.

It did not turn out to be quite that easy. When Japanese picket boats spotted Vice-Admiral William Halsey's naval task force 650 miles (1,046km) off Japan, Halsey gave the *Hornet*'s captain, Marc Mitscher, the launch order. In *Early Launch*, Doolittle appears in the center wearing a yellow life preserver and talking to the *Hornet*'s launch officer; Doolittle's co-pilot has his hand on the plane. There was less than 500 feet (152m) of runway in front of Doolittle's

plane, and with seas cresting at thirty feet (9m), timing each plane's take-off run to coincide with the *Hornet*'s bow rise was critical. When the deck officer signaled, Doolittle would release his brakes, the deck crew would remove the chocks under the plane's tires, and the B-25 would lumber into the air, assisted by the rising deck. Doolittle's right wing would clear the carrier's superstructure by a mere six feet (2m).

The Doolittle Raiders
United States Army Air Force

Robert Taylor

ORIGINAL PLANNING BEHIND THE DOOLITTLE RAID HAD THE B-25S BOMBING JAPAN BY night and landing in China at first light. Instead, the bombers took off from the *Hornet* before 9:30 A.M. and were over Tokyo by lunchtime. Coincidentally, a practice air raid drill had recently ended and air defense crews had just lowered the city's barrage balloons, which were designed to defend against low altitude bombing. When Doolittle's raiders appeared over the city flying below 1,000 feet (305m), many Japanese assumed the planes were part of the drill and waved to the B-25s.

Thirteen planes were to bomb targets in and around Tokyo; three more were to hit sites in Osaka, Nagoya, and Kobe. Robert Taylor's *The Doolittle Raiders* focuses on the planes that went to Nagoya. In the foreground, Major John Hilger, the group's executive officer, flies southward in the fourteenth plane to take off from the *Hornet*. Hilger's bomb bay doors are still open, and he may be headed towards his next target. On the river below, Japanese fishermen can be seen going about their business. Lieutenant William Farrow's plane, the sixteenth to take off, flies above Hilger's B-25. Lieutenant George Barr, Farrow's navigator, described seeing "smoke and fire"—the result of previous bombing by Hilger and Lieutenant Donald Smith, whose number fifteen plane does not appear in the painting. Anti-aircraft shells burst over Hilger and Smith's targets. Barr describes the scene: "Hilger's plane was flying in a southerly direction and at a lower altitude than ours. (We were at fifteen hundred feet [457m].) Then we realized the Japs were firing at him and coming close to us, since we were crossing his line of flight."

B-25 Doolittle Raid

United States Army Air Force

Keith Ferris

KEITH FERRIS DEPICTS THE ESCAPE OF CAPTAIN C. ROSS GREENING'S B-25 FROM TWO Japanese Mitsubishi A6M Zeros. The B-25, *Hari Karier*, was the eleventh plane to take off from the *Hornet*. Greening's targets were oil refineries between Tokyo and Yokohama. Northeast of Tokyo, four fighters closed in on *Hari Karier*, but Sergeant Melvin Gardner in the top turret hit two of them, discouraging the others. After Greening had climbed to 1,200 feet (366m) to escape the blast effects of his bombing, Staff Sergeant William L. Birch, the bombardier, released his remaining bombs over a large oil refinery's gasoline tanks. At that point, Greening headed for China flying at fifty feet (15m).

Eleven of the sixteen planes came close to reaching the China coast, but they had all run out of gas. As a result of fuel shortages, eleven of the crews bailed out in the dark over China, a few ditched at sea, and one crew landed in Russia and was interned there. The Japanese captured eight crewmen, who were tried for war crimes on charges of shooting up a school playground. Arrived at by torture, their confessions were written in Japanese, which the Americans could not read. The Japanese executed three, tying them to a cross in a mocking imitation of Christ. The other five later had their death sentences commuted to life in prison. For the poor Chinese who had aided the Doolittle raiders, the Japanese replayed the Rape of Nanking, this time killing 250,000 men, women, and children in Chekiang and Kiangsi provinces.

The attack on Tokyo proved a great embarrassment to the Japanese military, and to protect the Emperor, four fighter squadrons were recalled from China. To prevent more carrier raids against the home islands, the Japanese high command approved the invasion of Midway, which led to the loss of four Japanese aircraft carriers and proved to be the turning point of the War in the Pacific.

As a result of his leadership during the bombing of Japan in April 1942, Doolittle was promoted from lieutenant colonel to brigadier general by President Franklin D. Roosevelt; he was never a colonel. He finished World War II as a lieutenant general, the highest-ranking reserve officer in the army. Doolittle held a doctorate in advanced engineering from MIT and after the war he resigned from the army to work for Shell Oil, where he helped develop 100-octane aviation fuel.

Mareeba Maintenance

United States Army Air Force

Paul Eckley

In November 1941, one month before the War in the Pacific began, General Douglas MacArthur sent Major General Lewis Brereton to Australia. Brereton's job was to acquire airfields through which the Army Air Corps could ferry bombers to the Philippine Islands. Taking him to Queensland on Australia's northeast coast, an RAAF (Royal Australian Air Force) officer showed him Townsville, a small town of 25,000 people connected to Brisbane by a railroad with a single set of tracks. The Army Corps of Engineers was soon working on airfields south of Townsville at Woodstock and Charters Towers, which would serve as bases from which to work later. One hundred miles (161km) north up the Coral Sea coast, Brereton picked out a site for a base at Mareeba, some twenty miles (32km) inland from Cairns.

Mareeba became home to the 19th Bomb Group. In the early days of 1942, the group staged missions against the Japanese naval base at Rabaul on New Britain, flying through Port Moresby on the southeast coast of New Guinea.

The flight from Mareeba to Port Moresby was 540 miles (869km), and it was an equal distance from Port Moresby to Rabaul. All told, the round trip was 1,100 miles (1,770km). Seldom did the 19th Bomb Group send more than nine B-17s on a mission, but these raids on Rabaul provided valuable reconnaissance and forestalled any surprise attacks from the Japanese navy.

Lieutenant Paul Eckley, a flyer in the 19th Bomb Group, made a sketch for *Mareeba Maintenance* in the summer of 1942. This watercolor depicts a ground crew replacing propellers and engines on *Tojo's Physic*, a B-17E model. There were few facilities or spare parts at Mareeba, and no luxuries. Here, a mechanic works on an engine from a two-by-four platform adjacent to a bent propeller, which would be salvaged, as all parts were, for later use. In front of the right wing, the ground crew gathers to replace engines, a time-consuming, complicated procedure. The engine hoist appears in the background as a moveable scaffold.

Howell Walker of National Geographic photographed Lieutenant Paul Eckley painting a watercolor sketch for Mareeba Maintenance on site in Mareeba, Northern Queensland, Australia, in the summer of 1942. The photo appeared in the magazine early in 1943 and Walker presented Eckley with a copy of this picture among others. Eckley had painted the sketch on a piece of cardboard, which he later gave to a distant cousin. Using Walker's photograph, Eckley was able to recreate the original painting of *Mareeba Maintenance*.

B-29s Over Japan

United States Army Air Force

Jim Dietz

Jim Dietz depicts a high altitude attack, with both the Zeros and the 489th Bomb Group flying through Japanese flak. Despite the blackened sky, the attack took place during the day, and the sun can be seen reflected in the Zeros and the Superfortresses, as well as in the clouds behind *Joltin' Josie*. One B-29's right outboard engine is on fire and is going down, along with one of the Zeros. During one raid on Nagoya in January 1945, Japanese fighters made more than 900 passes at the B-29s, including ramming (or kamikaze) attempts.

The flanks of *Joltin' Josie*, also known as *The Pacific Pioneer*, featured a Vargas-like girl wearing high heels, a loincloth, and a raccoon hat, and carrying a frontier rifle, powder horn, and Bowie knife. It was *Josie* that brought Brigadier (later Major) General Haywood S. Hansell, Jr. to Saipan in October 1944. One of the authors of the American strategic bombing doctrine and the recently commissioned head of XXI Bomber Command, Twentieth Air Force, Hansell hoped to knock out Japan's industries with precision daylight bombing. Unfortunately, the weather and the jet stream over Japan completely frustrated his efforts. In February 1945, General H.H. "Hap" Arnold, commanding the Twentieth from Washington, replaced Hansell with Major General Curtis E. LeMay. Arnold wanted results and was not above area bombing Nagoya's aircraft industry with incendiaries. His strategy was ultimately successful. Repeated attacks on Nagoya destroyed the aircraft factories, clogged the streets, and ruined the dispersal plans that were supposed to help safeguard Japanese production against American bombing.

Final Assault

United States Army Air Force

Stan Stokes

ALTHOUGH THIS PAINTING IS SET DURING THE DAY, STAN STOKE'S *FINAL ASSAULT* demonstrates the futility of Japanese night-fighters. The Japanese aircraft is a Kawasaki Ki-45, a two-engine night-fighter capable of 340 miles per hour (547 kph). With a ceiling of 35,000 feet (10,668m), it was able to climb to the altitude of cruising B-29s. The Ki-45 depicted wears the colors of the 53rd Sentai, a ramming unit. Here, the Ki-45, called *Toryu* (Dragon Slayer), meets its end at the hands of *Lady Mary Anna* from the 498th Bomb Group.

The demise of the Ki-45 was typical. In his memoir, *Superfortress*, General LeMay maintained that although Japanese night-fighters tangled with his bomber crews, he had no evidence that one had ever shot down a B-29. Contemptuous of the night-fighters, LeMay took the guns out of the B-29s in March 1945 and ordered low-level night attacks.

Gunning in a B-29 was already a difficult task. Since the B-29 was pressurized, it had to have remote-controlled guns; individual gun turrets were too difficult to pressurize. The B-29 had four turrets top and bottom, each containing two .50-caliber machine guns with 1000 rounds per gun, as well as a manned tail position with a 20mm, 100-round cannon. Later, two more guns were added to the forward dorsal turret. The central fire control gunner and the two waist gunners were located just forward of the national insignia. Three of the gunners looked out of plexiglass bubbles for observation, but the central gunner could fire any two of the guns simultaneously. Computer-assisted gun sights, aided by gyroscopes, locked on to an approaching plane's wings and fed speed, altitude, and distance information to the gunners. A safety lockout switch prevented the guns from shooting any part of their own plane.

Toryu (Dragon Slayer)

United States Army Air Force

Jim Laurier

Toryu (Dragon Slayer) pictures an incident in the February 19, 1945 bombing campaign over Japan. A flight of B-29s from the 500th Bomb Group's 881st Squadron (out of Saipan's Isley Field) is bombing Tokyo. In addition to flak, the Japanese are attacking with Tonys, Zekes, and Nicks. Tony was the American name for the plane in the upper right, a Kawasaki Ki-61 *Hein* (Swallow), which had the only liquid-cooled engine in the Japanese fighter inventory. The Zeke is the Zero at the lower right. The Nick is the twin-engine Kawasaki Ki-45 flown by Lieutenant Kenji Yamada of the 53rd Sentai Squadron. In a ramming (kamikaze) maneuver, Yamada cut $Z^2 12$ of the 881st in half. Although six members of the eleven-man Ki-45 crew were able to parachute out (one man's parachute caught fire and burned up), Lieutenant Yamada died.

One month earlier, Japan's Supreme Council for the Direction of the War had made such suicide attacks government policy. Many Japanese equated the Special Attack Forces, notably the Kamikaze, with falling cherry blossoms, offering beauty in their deaths. Hino Ashihei, a famous Japanese poet, compared their deaths to the "fire-arrow deities" who sacrificed themselves to cleanse an impure world. The 53rd Sentai Squadron painted their planes with the arrow of the fire-arrow gods. Masaki Hiroshi, a liberal intellectual, published a small journal critical of the sacrifice depicted here, as well as the suicide submarines and human torpedoes. "Spirit," Hiroshi wrote, "is being used as a substitute for material. Is this any way to treat human beings?" Curiously, the authoritarian Japanese regime never arrested Hiroshi.

Raid on the China Coast
United States Army Air Force

Roy Grinnell

THE FALCON IS A BIRD OF PREY. IN THE MIDDLE AGES THE NOBILITY TRAINED FALCONS TO kill ducks. Below this falcon the Japanese ship off the coast of China is a sitting duck. The B-25 is the *Lady Lil* of the 498th Bomb Squadron, "The Falcons." The pilot, Lieutenant Albert J. Beiga, named the plane for his girlfriend, and the mission took place April 1945 between Amoy and Swatow, due west of Formosa. Grinnell has painted the most striking plane in the squadron, which was part of the 345th Bomb Group, known as the "Air Apaches," as indicated by the Indian's head on the rear stabilizer.

Beginning in August 1942, there were a number of eccentric innovators within the Fifth Air Force, then under the command of Major General George Kenney. One genuinely unusual figure was Major Paul "Pappy" Gunn, a former flight instructor for Philippine Air Lines. Made a captain at age forty, Gunn had a knack for making clever field modifications. He set to work increasing the fire power on American medium bombers, starting with the Douglas A-20. But his *magnum opus* was the B-25.

Certain that lowering the altitude of the B-25 would increase the destruction, Gunn practiced strafing and blowing up ships starting at 150 feet (46m). Convinced the bombardier was superfluous, Gunn got rid of him, along with the plane's lower turret. In their place, he added up to eight .50-caliber machine guns in the nose of the B-25, which the pilot fired from his control yoke. One B-25 variant even sported a 75mm cannon, but the recoil proved to be too hard on the air frame. Gunn's B-25s could drop a 500-pound (227kg) bomb with a five second delayed-action fuse into a ship the size of the one seen in *Raid on the China Coast* and blow out its bottom. The planes were deadly, shredding everything above deck, including sailors and antiaircraft guns.

Pacific Dolls

United States Army Air Force

Stan Stokes

AFTER RETURNING FROM A MISSION OVER JAPAN, *TEXAS DOLL* OF THE 497TH BOMB GROUP stands on its tricycle landing gear at Saipan's Isley Field. Empty, this behemoth weighed 74,500 pounds (33,793kg), more than twice as much as a B-17. The crew of the *Texas Doll* flew in a pressurized cabin and even had a food warmer so they could have a hot dinner on return flights. The Boeing B-29 Super-fortress was an immensely complicated machine with a computerized, remote-control gun system and 125 electrical motors, which required a supplemental gasoline-powered generator in the rear of the aircraft to meet their power needs. Looking at all the switches and dials, one B-29 engineer notably wondered how he would ever learn it all. He eventually did learn it, but only after virtually memorizing the manual. According to army aptitude tests, aircrews were statistically the smartest men in the United States Army. They had to be.

The navigator of *Texas Doll*, Lieutenant Colonel Don Julin, wrote a memoir about the crew's experiences. In *Flying the Red Carpet*, he describes seeing B-29s crash on take-off and collide mid-air in front of him. The closest call Colonel Edward Cutler's crew personally had came on their first mission, when a Japanese 20mm cannon shell hit their bomb bay. Although the blast's concussion deformed one of their gas tanks, it thankfully did not ignite it. *Texas Doll* took part in the "Tokyo firestorm" raids on the nights of March 9–10, 1945, when General LeMay ordered all but the B-29s' tail guns, as well as their armor, removed to leave room for more incendiaries. *Texas Doll* survived thirty-six missions over Japan.

Beginning of the End
United States Army Air Force

William S. Phillips

IN THE EARLY MORNING HOURS OF AUGUST 6, 1945, THE ISLAND OF IWO JIMA LIES OFF to the right of the *Enola Gay*. Mount Suribachi, where the Marines had famously raised the American flag, rises from the far end of the island. Before the plane could release its devastating payload over Hiroshima, Iwo Jima had demanded its own reckoning. From airfields on the island, Japanese fighters had continually attacked B-29s on their way to Japan from Saipan, causing the bombers to give it a wide berth. Often, this meant the crews ran out of gas and had to ditch in the ocean.

To give the bombers a freer hand, the Marines invaded Iwo Jima on February 19, 1945. The entire 21,000 man Japanese garrison fought to the death, although for the first time, they inflicted more casualties on the Americans than they suffered. More than 6,000 Marines died, with an additional 20,000 wounded.

Given the aggression the Japanese demonstrated at Iwo Jima and later at Okinawa, where 49,000 Americans were killed and wounded, President Harry S. Truman made the difficult decision to bring the war to an end through the

use of atomic weapons. General Arnold handpicked Colonel Paul W. Tibbets, Jr., to command the 509th Bomb Group, which would drop the atomic bombs. For the August 6th run, Tibbets used a subordinate's plane, which he renamed for his mother, *Enola Gay*. After the war, the famous plane was stored at the National Archives.

In May 1995, the bomber's restored forward fuselage and other parts of the plane were brought out of storage and displayed at the Smithsonian Institution's National Air and Space Museum in an exhibit commemorating the end of World War II. Originally, the plane was to be presented as part of a larger interpretive exhibit focusing on the horrors of atomic weapons, but the proposed exhibit was canceled due to what was perceived as its unbalanced editorial bias. Replaced by the less complicated, more evenhanded display (which went on to become one of the Smithsonian's most popular ever), the controversial, canceled exhibit and the passionate feelings it aroused highlight the ambivalence that still exists with regard to the use of atomic weapons against Japan.

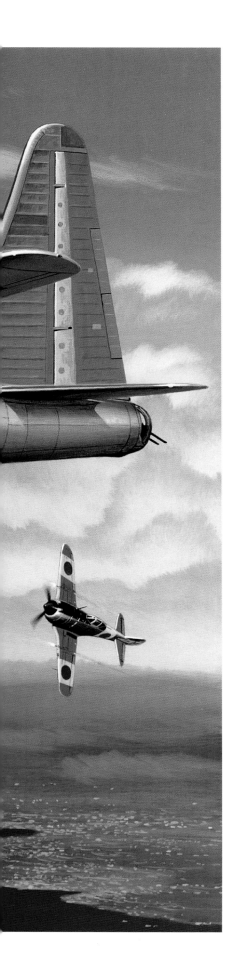

The Hobo Queens

United States Army Air Force

Stan Stokes

WHEN THE ARMY AIR CORPS (LATER FORCES) WANTED TO REPLACE THE B-17 AND B-24 with a super heavy bomber, both Boeing and Consolidated developed proto-types. The Army Air Forces never ordered enough B-32 Dominators from Consolidated to justify mass production, though. Consolidated built just one hundred, and only fifteen were ever operational. Essentially a super-Liberator, the B-32 had a pressurized cabin, remote control gunnery, and reversible pitch propellers that allowed it to slow down upon landing. Most noticeable was its ski jump tail. Had the B-32 ever been mass-produced, it would have made the B-24 look sleek by comparison. No one wanted these planes until General George Kenney convinced General Arnold to let him test them in action, lead-ing to the establishment of the 312th Bomb Group's 386th Squadron, based at Yontan, Okinawa.

In the closing days of the war, the Dominators attacked an alcohol distillery on Formosa to prevent the Japanese from using the alcohol as fuel. After the August 6, 1945 atomic drop on Hiroshima, followed three days later by the bombing of Nagasaki, these two B-32 Dominators were flying an unescorted photographic mission over Tokyo. At 20,000 feet (6,096m), Japanese fighters attacked both the *Hobo Queen* and the *Hobo Queen II*. On the fighters' first pass, cannon rounds depressurized the *Hobo Queen*, forcing pilot Lieutenant John R. Anderson to dive 10,000 feet (3,048m) for breathable air. The Zeros also wounded the gunners in the rear of the plane, and despite his own wounds, Sergeant Joseph Lacherite had to administer first aid to Sergeants John T. Houston and Anthony J. Marchione. On their second pass, the Japanese fighters mortally wounded Marchione, who may have been the last Army Air Forces war casualty. The *Hobo Queens* claimed three Japanese fighters shot down, but the *Hobo Queen* was riddled with bullet holes. Anderson had to land it with one of its propellers feathered. The next day, two white-painted Japanese Bettys carrying Japanese peace envoys landed at Ie Shima, just off Okinawa. By August 19, 1945, the Japanese ceased attacks on American aircraft.

About the Artists

Robert Bailey

Even as a small boy, Robert Bailey was always drawing and painting aircraft. Born and raised in England, where he attended the College of Art in Stoke-on-Trent, Straffordshire, he was originally inspired by his father, who often told exciting tales of battles in North Africa and Italy. Most boys growing up in England in the shadow of World War II were avid readers of *Commando* comics, and Robert was no exception. He has amassed a large collection of these comics plus more than eighty books on the fictional fighter pilot "Biggles." He also owns an impressive library of books on military and aviation history as well as a large collection of model airplanes that he uses as additional visual data. Bailey is an Artist Fellow with the American Society of Aviation Artists and a member of the Canadian Aviation Artists Association. His prints and originals are sold worldwide, including in the U.S., Australia, Canada, Great Britain, and Germany.

For information or to order prints, call or write:
Bailey Art and Publishing, Inc.
4 Brightbank Avenue
Stony Plain, Alberta, Canada T7Z 1G6
tel: (780) 963-5480
fax: (780) 963-7193
e-mail: bailart@telusplanet.net
www.telusplanet.net/public/bailart

Gil Cohen

For more than forty years, Gil Cohen has worked as a freelance illustrator and painter of historical subjects. A graduate of the Philadelphia College of Art (now the University of the Arts), his clients include the U.S. Information Agency, the National Park Service, Paramount Pictures, the U.S. Coast Guard, and Boeing and Sikorsky Aircraft Companies. Artist Fellow Cohen is a three-time Best of Show winner at American Society of Aviation Artists (ASAA) juried exhibitions, and is the recipient of the British Guild of Aviation Artists' Best of Show by an American artist. His paintings have been exhibited at the New York Society of Illustrators, at the Kennedy Center in Washington, D.C., at a one-man show at the Mighty Eighth Heritage Museum in Savannah, GA, and at numer-

ous Civil War battlefield memorial parks. His painting *Staying Power/Berlin* 1948-49 was presented to the Berlin Airlift Museum. For several years, he served on the Board of Directors of the New York-based Society of Illustrators, where he chaired the Government Services Program. Gil Cohen's studio is located in the home that he shares with his wife, Alice, in historic Doylestown, Pennsylvania.

For information or to order prints, call or write:
Gil Cohen
62 Creek Drive
Doylestown, PA 18901-4717
tel: (215) 348-0779
fax: (215) 348-2746
e-mail: gilcoart@pil.net

Jim Dietz

For Jim Dietz, simply illustrating aviation hardware is not presenting the whole picture; he prefers to add a human element to truly capture the moment in his paintings. "The people, settings, and costumes are what make aviation history exciting and romantic to me," says the artist. A graduate of the Art Center College of Design, he worked as a commercial illustrator in Los Angeles before moving to Seattle to pursue a career in aviation art. His clients include Boeing, Bell Helicopter, Allison, and the Flying Tigers. His work has been honored with several gold medals from the Los Angeles Society of Illustrators and was voted Best of Show in three successive years in the Experimental Aircraft Association Aviation Art Show. His work has been exhibited in museums throughout the country, including the Experimental Aircraft Association Museum, the San Diego Air Museum, and the Smithsonian Institution's National Air and Space Museum. Dietz lives in Seattle with his wife, Patti, and their Australian Shepherd, Tazzy, who is often seen in Jim's paintings.

For information or to order prints, call or write:
James Dietz
2203 13th Avenue East
Seattle, WA 98102
tel: (206) 325-1151
fax: (206) 325-1151
e-mail: dietzart@aol.com

Paul Eckley

Paul Eckley has had his head and heart in the sky for as long as he can remember. His first flight was in a J-1 Standard with the Gates Flying Circus at Ithaca, New York in 1927. After graduating from the Pratt Institute School of Art and Design in Brooklyn, Eckley enlisted in the US Army Aviation Cadets and graduated from flying school five days after the bombing of Pearl Harbor. He served in the South Pacific, flying bomber missions from Australia and New Guinea as a member of the 19th Bomb Group. Each of Eckley's paintings tells a story, often one witnessed firsthand by the artist himself. His combat experiences have inspired him to document the efforts of the US Army Air Corps during the first year of the war in the Pacific. In addition to being a pilot, Eckley directed graphic arts facilities for the remainder of his twenty-four years of active duty in the Air Force. His last assignment was Director of Graphic Arts at the Joint Chiefs of Staff at the Pentagon in Washington, D.C., where he prepared briefing materials for the Chairman of the Joint Chiefs and the Secretary of Defense for their appearances at the White House and before Congressional committees. Eckley's paintings have appeared in the EAA Air Adventure Museum at Oshkosh, Wisconsin, in the Museum of Naval Aviation at Pensacola, Florida, and in corporate offices and private collections around North America. He is an Artist Member of the American Society of Aviation Artists.

For information or to order prints, call or write:
Paul W. Eckley
2695 Augusta Drive North
Clearwater, FL 33761
tel: (727) 797-1705
e-mail: eckstudio@aol.com
www.eckleyaviationart.com

Keith Ferris

The son of a career air force officer, Keith Ferris nurtured his love for aeronautics while growing up on military bases throughout the United States. As a freelance aviation artist and founding member of the

American Society of Aviation Artists (ASAA), he has been serving the advertising, editorial, public relations, and historical documentation needs of the aviation community for more than fifty years. His clients have included most major aerospace corporations, associations, and publications. A life member of the Air Force Association, he was a recipient of its Citation of Honor in 1978 for his art and its special award in 1985 for his lifetime of air force history documentation. Ferris paintings have been judged Best of Show at ASAA's annual exhibitions in 1995, 1996, 1999, and 2000. Best known for his seventy-five-foot (22.8m) murals *Fortresses Under Fire* and *The Evolution of Jet Aviation*, his work has been exhibited at the Smithsonian Institution in Washington, D.C. and the United States Air Force Academy in Colorado Springs, Colorado. In 1992, he was inducted into the Aviation Hall of Fame of New Jersey, joining such aviation legends as Amelia Earhart and Charles Lindbergh. Keith Ferris lives with his wife, Peggy, in Morris Plains, New Jersey, where he maintains a large reference library dedicated to aeronautics.

For information or to order prints, call or write:
Keith Ferris Inc.
50 Moraine Road
Morris Plains, NJ 07950-2750
tel: (973) 539-3363
fax: (973) 605-1863
e-mail: kferris303@aol.com
www.keithferrisart.com

Nixon Galloway

With an extensive background in aviation and more than fifty years of experience as an artist, Nixon "Nick" Galloway is an experienced professional who is well known for the broad scope of work he has produced for corporations and, more recently, the prints and the paintings he has created for galleries and individual commissions. His paintings are held in many private collections and have been exhibited at the Air Force Museum, the Smithsonian Air and Space Museum, the Kennedy Space Center, the EAA Museum, the RAF Museum in London, and the White House. The U.S. Air Force art collection includes more than thirty of his paintings. Galloway is an Artist Fellow member and a past president of the American Society of Aviation Artists. When not working in his studio, he can often

be found on the ski slopes or racing his sailboat in southern California.

For information or to order prints, call or write:
Nixon Galloway
Studio G, Inc.
755 Marine Avenue
Manhattan Beach, CA 90266
tel: (310) 545-7709
fax: (310) 545-7096
e-mail: asaartist@aol.com
www.nixongallowayartist.com

Henry Godines

For more than twenty-five years, Henry Godines has captured in oil the action and drama of aerial combat in vivid and historically accurate detail. A self-taught artist, he imbues his exacting realistic approach with touches of spontaneity that bring his subjects to life. His paintings have received a number of awards, including the Award of Merit at the 1995 SimuFlite/Flying Magazine Horizons of Flight Competition in Dallas, Texas, and Honorable Mention at both the All Media Exhibit in Irvine, California and the 1992 ASAA Exhibit in San Diego, California. He is a member of the American Society of Aviation Artists and the Orange County Latino Artist Network. Originally from south Texas, Godines now resides in southern California.

For information or to order prints, call or write:
Avant-Garde Publishing
Henry Godines
P.O. Box 809
Midway City, CA 92655
tel: (714) 898-7598
e-mail: hgodines@earthlink.net
www.home.earthlink.net/~hgodines/

Roy Grinnell

Capturing aviation history on canvas is Roy Grinnell's forte, and it has brought him worldwide recognition as an aviation artist of the highest caliber. His documentation of aerial combat events has earned him the honor of being the official artist for the American Fighter Aces Association and the Confederate Air Force. In addition, he has done commissioned prints for the Association of Naval Aviation, the Air Force, the National

Aviation Hall of Fame in Dayton, Ohio, and the Flying Tigers Association. Roy's camaraderie with legendary pilots has allowed him to carve an impressive niche in aviation art history in the form of prints and publications. His art has appeared in editions of *Naval Aviation News*, *The Foundation Journal*, *Aviation History* and *The Flight Journal*. He is a member of the Skyhawk Association, the American Society of Aviation Artists, the American Fighter Aces Association, the Confederate Air Force, and the Sino-American Aviation Heritage Foundation, and co-founder of the Institute of Pacific Aircraft Research. Roy was the recent recipient of the prestigious R.G. Smith Excellence in Aviation Art Award, given by the US Navy in Pensacola, Florida.

For information or to order prints, call or write:
Keep 'em Flying-Tiger Bay
1100 Mill Run
Allen, TX 75002
tel: (972) 727-6045, ext. 3
e-mail: roygrinnell@aol.com; buywrbonds@aol.com

Jim Laurier

For Jim Laurier, the love of art and airplanes have combined to create a fulfilling career. Laurier, graduate of the Paier School of Art in Hamden, Connecticut, has flown a wide assortment of aircraft, lending him extensive knowledge of the ways in which they operate. He is well known for his ability to combine technical accuracy with a realistic depiction of the aircraft in motion. His clients include the U.S. Air Force, the Aircraft Owners and Pilots Association, and World War II and Aviation History magazines. His work has been exhibited all around the United States, winning top awards at several shows. Dedicated to his profession, he is a Fellow Member and Trustee of the American Society of Aviation Artists, and a member of the New York Society of Illustrators, the American Fighter Aces Association, and the Air Force Art Program. Laurier lives in Keene, New Hampshire with his wife, Jill, where he produces electronic art and publishes prints.

For information or to order prints, call or write:
Aviation Art by Jim Laurier
P.O. Box 1118
Keene, NH 03431
tel: (603) 357-2051
fax: (603) 357-4451
www.aviation-art.simplenet.com

William S. Phillips

As long as he can remember, Bill Phillips has had a love affair with flight, and his aviation art conveys his passion to the viewer. An experienced pilot, Phillips has logged hours in F-106s, F-15s, and RF-4s, and has spent a tour of duty in the Air Force, which included an assignment at Tan Son Nhut, Vietnam. There, he spent many afternoons sketching the various aircraft on the base and the beautiful clouds that would gather during the monsoon season. Phillips' work hangs in numerous public and private collections throughout the world. In June of 1987, he was given a one-man retrospective at the National Air and Space Museum in Washington, D.C.— one of only a few artists to be so honored. The show was so popular that it toured North America for four years. In 1991, one of Phillips' works received the "History Award" as part of "Art for the Parks," the prestigious annual fund-raiser for the National Park Service. And, in July of 1997, the U.S. Postal Service released a twenty-stamp sheet depicting "Classic American Aircraft" that Phillips had been commissioned to paint.

For information or to order prints, call or write:
William S. Phillips Fine Art
P.O. Box 677
Ashland, OR 97520
tel: (541) 482-8093
fax: (541) 482-1157

Stan Stokes

For more than twenty-five years, Stan Stokes has been depicting the world's greatest aircraft. Stokes' attention to detail and his superb illustrative techniques, especially his gift for creating three-dimensional effects, have made a name for the California artist. "Incredibly accurate" is a common description of a Stokes painting. His talent not going unnoticed, he received the Benedictine Art Award and First place in the Smithsonian Institute's National Air and Space Museum Golden Age of Flight Art Competition in 1984. His original paintings adorn many of the nation's most famous aviation museums, including the National Air and Space Museum, the Air Force Museum in Dayton, Ohio, and the Museum of Naval Aviation in Pensacola, Florida. From 1985–1991, he produced fourteen paintings for NASA's art collection. In May 2000, Stokes was presented the R.G. Smith Award for Excellence in Naval Aviation Art by the National Museum of Naval Aviation Foundation.

For information or to order prints, call or write:
The Stokes Collection
26352 Carmel Rancho Lane, Suite 105
Carmel, CA 93923
tel: (800) 359-4644

Robert Taylor

Robert Taylor has been painting and sketching since his early years and has earned a reputation that makes him one of today's leading aviation artists. His true talent lies in his ability to take viewers right into a scene, making it almost possible to smell the smoke of battle, or to experience the exhilaration of flight. In the mid-seventies, a noteworthy alliance with the Military Gallery led Taylor on his path to fame. His clients have included the British royal family, a former American president, legendary pilots and aircrews, and other aviation enthusiasts. His work has been featured on television programs and in newspaper and magazine articles. *The Washington Post* described his paintings and drawings as exuding "a lyrical and majestic quality." His one-man exhibition in London in 1983 was heavily covered by international media, as was his one-man exhibition at the Smithsonian Institution's National Air and Space Museum in Washington, D.C., seen by ten million visitors. The latter has been quoted as the most successful aviation art exhibit ever staged.

For information or to order prints, call or write:
Military Gallery/Universal Publishing Group
821 E. Ojai Avenue
Ojai, CA 93023
tel: (805) 640-0057
fax: (805) 640-0059
e-mail: milgallery@aol.com
www.universal-publishing.co.uk

Nicolas Trudgian

Arriving on the scene in the late 1980s, Nicolas Trudgian is a best-selling aviation artist who has generated artwork for some of the major auto and aerospace manufacturers. Described as a landscape artist who paints aircraft, he enjoys painting the machinery of yesteryear with brilliant colors and resolution. Upon joining the Military Gallery, his paintings were produced as prints for the first time, launching his career on an international scale. Today, the quality of his work is recognized around the world, making him one of the most popular aviation artists in the world. Trudgian lives and works in Gloucestershire, England.

For information or to order prints, call or write:
Military Gallery/Universal Publishing Group
821 E. Ojai Avenue
Ojai, CA 93023
tel: (805) 640-0057
fax: (805) 640-0059
e-mail: milgallery@aol.com
www.universal-publishing.co.uk

Keith Woodcock

After initially pursuing a career in technical illustration and graphic design, Keith Woodcock decided in 1982 to devote his energies and talents to painting aviation subjects full-time. Since then, he has become one of Britain's most respected artists in his field, exhibiting widely in the U.K., Europe, and in North America. His work has won many awards, including a Par Excellence award at the EAA Aviation Art Competition in Oshkosh, the prestigious Aviation Painting of the Year award at the Guild of Aviation Artist's annual London exhibition followed by the Best Oil Painting award at the same show three years later, the James V. Roy award at the annual American Society of Aviation Artist's annual exhibition, the Founders Award at the same show, and an ASAA Award of Merit in 1999. Woodcock's paintings have received critical acclaim for their atmosphere and authenticity, the latter often demanding extensive research. Many examples now hang in the permanent collections of museums, service establishments, aerospace companies, and private individuals worldwide. Virtually all his work is now specially commissioned.

For information or to order prints, call or write:
Keith Woodcock
2nd floor, Adelphi Mill
Grimshaw Lane
Bollington, Macclesfield
SK10 5JB
England
tel: 01625 576757
e-mail: info@keithwoodcock.com
www.keithwoodcock.com

Index

Photo Credits

Archive Photos: ©Horace Abrahams/ Keystone: 14, 73; ©Davis/ Topical Press Agency: 58

©C.S. Bailey: 10

©Robert Bailey: 26, 26-27, 32-33, 49, 50, 56-57, 86, 86-87

©Brown Brothers: 124

©Gil Cohen: 1, 36-37, 46-47, 48-49, 114-115

Corbis: © Bettmann: 8, 11 bottom, 40; ©Hulton-Deutsch Collection: 11 top, 77

©Jim Dietz: 6-7, 18, 52-53, 60-61, 110, 116-117, 120-121, 128-129

©Paul Eckley: 16, 119, 127

©Keith Ferris: 22-23, 75, 80, 92-93, 96-97, 112-113, 125, Back End Papers

©FPG: 12, 17, 93, 110-111, 121

©National Archives: 13, 18-19, 95

National Geographic: ©Howell Walker: 126

©Nixon Galloway: 24-25, 82-83

©Henry Godines: 94-95

©Roy Grinnell: 51, 66, 67, 98-99, 134-135

©Colin Heaton: 75

©Jim Laurier: 102-103, 132-133

©William S. Phillips: Front End Papers, 28-29, 30, 42-43, 54-55, 64-65, 70-71, 81, 84-85, 100-101, 137

©Stan Stokes: 31, 34-35, 62-63, 74, 88-89, 90-91, 106, 130-131, 136, 138-139

©Robert Taylor: 20-21, 38-39, 72-73, 76-77, 108-109, 118-119, 122-123

©Nicolas Trudgian: 2-3, 44-45, 78-79, 104-105

©Keith Woodcock: 40-41, 58-59, 68-69, 107

Digital Imaging, Daniel J. Rutkowski: 14, 16, 26, 40, 49, 58, 73, 75, 77, 86, 119, 126